Loving What Is

Loving What Is

YOU ARE ENOUGH

By Bela Fayth

First Printing 2019

23 22 21 20 19   5 4 3 2 1

ISBN: 978-1-946195-51-7

Library of Congress Control Number: 2019916902

Cover Photo by: Photographer is Sally Butler, La Vie Photography

Printed in the United States
Published by FuzionPress
1250 E 115th Street, Burnsville, MN 55337

Cover design and interior formatting by Ann Aubitz
FuzionPress.com

To my younger self and those like her:
YOU ARE ENOUGH!

ACKNOWLEDGEMENTS

I would first like to thank my mom and dad for making me who I am today. Thank you for walking by my side through life. Through every situation in my life, good and bad, you have always loved me where I was at. I am so thankful for that. Thank you for constantly giving me space to feel, talk about, and work through my feelings. You've taught me how to be graceful and given me the tools to be the best version of myself possible. Lastly, thank you for instilling in me a gracious, God-loving heart and teaching me that impact and giving back are essential in life.

Next off I would like to thank my siblings for teaching me patience, and for letting me be myself. I am so thankful that you all love to be goofy with me. I can't imagine life without your bickering, dancing, singing, and movie quotes.

A big thank you to my extended family, grandparents, aunts and uncles, and my little cousins for always reminding me how loved and important I am. I thank you for supporting me and encouraging me to chase my dreams no matter how crazy they may seem.

I would like to thank Steph Gold for taking me in as her youngest client. I am so thankful for you and your encouragement in my life.

I am so grateful for both of my therapists always listening to me rant and giving me space to work through hard things in my life. I would not be where I am without your listening ears or million-dollar advice.

Thank you to my editor, Berit Coleman, for taking the time out of your day to help make this book the best it can be. I appreciate all of your feedback and hard work put into this.

Thank you to Bethlehem Academy School for helping me get back on me feet and breathe life into me. The staff and environment played a crucial role in healing hurts and giving me opportunities to chase my dreams. I cherish my time spent at the school.

I am so thankful for the few true friends that I have in my life. You have made losing those close to me a little easier, and the wait for true friends, worth it.

Thank you to Cole and Sanja Hatter and the Thrive Connect community for pushing me to be my best self and to think bigger. Your love and support has made a world of difference in my life and I will never be able to thank you enough.

Thank you, Sarah Pendrick, for taking the time to write an amazing foreword and for the impact you make on women's lives each and every day. I aspire to make as big of an impact as you do every day.

Lastly, I thank you. The reader. I spent hours dreaming and working towards a book that I am proud to share with you. You reading this means I have made my dream a reality and I could not have done it without you. I hope something in this book will help you in your journey to be who you were created to be.

TABLE OF CONTENTS

FOREWORD

By Sarah Pendrick

A few years ago, I was told about this beautiful, empowering young woman whose mission was supporting other girls. Part of my mission has always been leading women to believe in themselves, and I've dedicated much of my life to mentoring and inspiring the next generation of women leaders. I had heard about this young leader that everyone had said I just had to meet. In walks Bela, she was everything that people had told me and within minutes of someone bringing her up to meet me I knew she was on this planet to make an impact.

Bela's heart, dedication, and passion spoke to me within minutes of our conversation. I saw much of my journey in her, and I knew she would be making a mark on this world. She continued to surprise me with her dedication and commitment to doing whatever she had to in order to grow, learn, and let others know that they are not alone.

In this book, Bela connects with you through sharing her struggles, challenges, and personal stories about the challenges that young women face, every day. She really connects you to and supports you in knowing that you are not alone. Bela offers you a step-by-step guide to overcoming rejection and bullying, how to handle the "haters," and move into forgiveness while empowering you at the same time. She shows you what loving yourself means and takes you on a journey of acceptance and love. She taps into what it looks like to use positive self-talk and shares with you tangible tips and exercises to use daily to create your ultimate happiness without needing anyone else's stamp of approval but your own.

Bela has structured this book with the perfect combination of storytelling, honesty, journaling exercises, and support for you on your journey of empowerment.

As young girls and women we have a responsibility to lift each other up and become our best selves. It starts with us. Choosing to go on this journey of self-love and to spread to others that they are not alone is what brings us all closer to each other and our dreams.

- Sarah Pendrick
International speaker, women empowerment leader and founder of The GirlTalk Network

CHAPTER ONE
Journaling

Journaling

Who are you?

_____

_____

_____

_____

_____

_____

Write a brief autobiography:

_____

_____

_____

_____

_____

_____

_____

Bela's Answers

My name is Iszabela, but I go by Bela. I am 19 years old. I am the oldest of 6 siblings, 2 of which I've never met. I live with my Mom, stepdad, 2 brothers, and a sister.

I recently graduated from High School. I enjoy spending my time listening to music, watching movies, Reading, journaling, and hanging out with friends and family.
My favorite color is Black.
My favorite food is Cucumbers with salt.
I love to laugh, quote movies, and dance.

I have found throughout my life that journaling has always been a safe place for me. It is what I do to get all of my feelings out without feeling or being interrupted or judged. I am free to write whatever I want and get it all out. Journaling has brought peace, clarity, and healing to my life. It has helped with my anxiety and depresssion. I can look back to where I was and see how far I have come. I can look back at the hurt and see my healing. I can look back at things I never thought I would be able to make it through. It is so cool to see the progress and remember situations that have grown me.

Throughout this book, I ask questions and leave space for you to journal your answers. I do this because journaling is a big part of my life and how I have gotten through situations, and I want to give that tool to you. This book is a safe place for you, and I want you to grow through it and write things down or highlight ideas that help or stand out to you. To get the most out of this book, journal and answer HONESTLY the questions I ask. Now obviously I cannot make you answer them, but at the very least, ponder the questions.

Tips

1. The most important thing is that you are HONEST when you journal: honest with yourself.

2. Make sure you put the date on the page so that you can look back.

3. Write about anything and everything: good things in your day, bad things, your feelings, what you want in life--- anything.

4. Don't put pressure on yourself; there is no right or wrong way to journal.

CHAPTER TWO

Expectations

> Expectations
>
> *noun*
>
> 1. something looked forward to, whether feared or hoped
> 2. an attitude of hope; anticipation

Imagine this... You have a really big secret that you don't want everyone to know. You have that nagging feeling inside that you just need to tell someone. You walk down the halls, feeling the weight of your secret, looking at people wondering if they somehow know. You finally decide that you are going to tell your best friend. You tell her it is top secret and that she CANNOT say anything to anyone. You tell her. You trust her. You feel relieved for a moment that IT is off your chest, but then the fear creeps in. What if she tells someone? What if the whole school finds out? What are you going to do?

In life, our expectations start at a very young age. In our minds, we generate expectations without even realizing it. Expectations are beliefs that something will happen; someone will do something or be a certain way. We also have expectations about what we may achieve.

We expect:

- to be held as babies
- to have food
- to have clothing
- to get birthday presents
- to go to school
- to get a job
- respect
- to have good teachers
- to like who we are
- our friends to be good friends
- adults to protect and guide us
- people to be there for us
- to have our secrets kept

Ideas to remember from this section:

1. What do you expect of others?

_____

_____

_____

_____

2. What do you expect of yourself?

_____

_____

_____

_____

3. Can you see any unmet expectations in your life?

_____

_____

_____

_____

Bela's Answers

1. I expect others to be respectful, honest, and kind to me.

2. I expect myself to be kind to all, always do my best, and to love and accept people for who they are.

3. I can see a few unmet expectations in my life. Not everyone I meet treats me how I want to be treated. I catch myself expecting others to have the same heart as me, which isn't realistic.

CHAPTER TWO.1

Disappointment

> Disappointment
> noun
> 1.   the feeling of sadness or displeasure caused
>   by the nonfulfillment of one's hopes or
>   expectations.

When our expectations are not lived up to, we feel disappointment. This is why it is so important to be able to sit and think about the expectations we have of ourselves and others. Some expectations are unrealistic; like asking a whale to climb a tree — never going to happen.

Remember that secret that you told your best friend? The one that, if it got out, would make you want to crawl under a rock and hide? You expected her to keep it. You trusted her.

Imagine this... the next day you walk into school. You're walking down the halls, and people are whispering to each other and looking at you. Some are even laughing. You wonder if maybe you have something in your teeth or stuck in your hair. You become self-conscious, and suddenly, your heart drops. You see your best friend, and she avoids you and avoids making eye contact. At that very moment, you know. She told.

You have to sit through classes knowing that everyone knows your secret. You walk down the halls with your head down, ignoring the snickers of those around you. You can't wait to get home to hide in your room.

You are disappointed in yourself for sharing something that you didn't want everyone to know in the first place. You are disappointed in your friend because you expected her to keep your secret.

Disappointment sometimes takes over for a little bit and makes us question who we can trust, and even if we can trust ourselves. Sometimes, as I said earlier, we tend to expect people who can't swim, to cross oceans for us. We sometimes expect something that will never happen. But what about the times when we have valid expectations of people? Valid expectations are expectations that are realistic that people should be able to meet. Sometimes even the simplest expectations are hard for some to meet like being a good friend, keeping plans, or keeping a secret.

Sometimes we expect so much of ourselves and others that it is impossible not to cause ourselves to be disappointed. When we free ourselves of expectations and let ourselves and those around us be who we are, and do our best, we have less pressure and are able to give and receive without strings attached. You will then be able to throw love and kindness like confetti, to everyone around you, and most importantly, to yourself.

Ideas to remember from this section:

1. Have you ever felt disappointed?

_____

_____

_____

_____

_____

_____

_____

2. Do you feel disappointed about something right now?

_____

_____

_____

_____

_____

_____

_____

_____

Bela's Answers

1. I have felt disappointment many times. It stings and hurts my feelings when things don't end up how I thought they would.

2. Right now as I am growing up, I am disappointed with how my relationship with my parents is progressing. We don't get along or communicate as well as we used to. We are all learning as time goes on, but I want things to get better.

CHAPTER TWO.2
Rejection

Rejection
noun
1. dismissing or refusing
the dismissal of a person's affections

The secret got out. Barely anyone looks at you or speaks to you. You walk the halls alone, heart pounding. You look at the floor to avoid eye contact. You sit by yourself at lunch and on the bus. No one is asking you to hang out over the weekend. You go home, sit in your room, and avoid talking to your family.

Finally, it is dinner time, and you look down and don't speak a single word except for when your mom asks how school was. All you have to say is, "fine." You barely eat anything, and then you lock yourself in your room and speak to no one for the rest of the night. You not only feel disappointed in yourself and your friend, but you feel like a total screw up. You feel like no one likes you or wants to be your friend. You feel rejection. Expectations are so impactful. Not only do they lead to disappointment, but they ultimately lead to the dreaded, all-consuming feeling of rejection. I am sure you have felt it before. It is that ball in your stomach that tightens. It is the lump in your throat.

It happens when you watch all of your friends hang out without you, or when you're telling your parents something you are proud of, and they brush it off. You feel it when you're wearing your favorite shirt and feeling super confident in an outfit, only to have someone tell you how ridiculous you look. It is feeling like you look really pretty in a picture, only to have someone tell you that you look gross. You feel it when you are really proud of something, and then someone comes in and points out everything that is wrong with it and why it isn't as good as you think it is. It's when others point out what is "wrong" with you and why you aren't as good as you think.

Rejection feels like no matter what you do, it is never good enough.

You may feel the need to "belong" and rejection is the feeling that you don't belong or matter anywhere. Rejection causes us to call ourselves names, talk down to ourselves, and feel gross about ourselves. We let others call us names and talk down to us as well. We think that because we have been left out--- that we are not good enough.

Rejection from Friends

The friend group that I was a part of for some of my years in school was the "popular" clique. You know that group where all the girls are nice to your face — but talk about you behind your back? The clique that liked to make fun of others who weren't in the group or were "different" than them? Yeah, that one. A lot of girls wanted to be accepted and be a part of our group, but what they did not know was that at lunch, whenever a girl in our clique was finished with her food and would get up to dump her tray, everyone still sitting would instantly start to talk bad about her. When the girl came back, the conversation was quickly hushed, and everyone would continue like best friends again.

It was as if the whole group was an illusion made up of people who actually didn't like each other or deep down didn't like who they were. I usually stayed quiet or sometimes tried to stand up for the girl they talked about, but I was looked at as the strange one—the one who didn't belong and had no right to tell them how to act. They looked at me like I didn't have permission to tell them that talking about others like that wasn't kind. Something inside of me longed for a good, true friend. I slowly started to realize that I could not find a true friend in that group.

Surprisingly, I "belonged" to the clique that bullied me. I played sports with these girls and was with them more than anyone else.

"Belonging" meant that:
- Puking noises were made when I walked into a room, making me feel like my mere existence disgusted them.
- My "friends" would invite everyone for a sleepover and leave me out.
- They would make plans in front of me, and act like I did not even exist.
- They wouldn't let me be in pictures with them because they said I was "too pretty."

While sometimes I felt like an arrow was above my head pointing at me saying "make fun of me," or "hurt me," other times I was overwhelmed with feeling invisible and alone. *I am not sure which feeling is more gut-wrenching.*

Rejection from Family

Another time in my life when I have felt rejection was when I was five-years-old. My birth dad decided he didn't want to be a dad anymore, so he moved to Arizona. Without saying goodbye. Ever since then, my birth dad rarely ever came home, maybe once or twice, if I was lucky. But, even when he did come back, *I was never a priority.* When he is home, he keeps busy with other people who take away the precious time he might spend with me. He spends maybe a day with me, and then fills the other days with golfing and visiting friends he hasn't seen in a while. He was never around for the hard, ugly parts of my life—nor the big, happy times.

My birth dad is half of me, but in some strange way, he is also a stranger to me. Seeing him so rarely, and all of the feelings I have towards him makes it very difficult to have a healthy father-daughter relationship, or honestly, any relationship at all. *Because of his lack of effort to be in my life, I always felt like I wasn't enough for him, and that I was unimportant.*

For the longest time I thought that *I* was the problem, I thought maybe if I would have been better, or smarter, or something, that he would have stayed, or my friends would have been better friends. But here is the harsh truth: *I cannot control other people's choices, and I cannot change them no matter how much I want to sometimes.* What people choose has nothing to do with me or you and everything to do with them. My birth dad leaving wasn't my fault; there is nothing I could have done that would have changed his mind. The girls not being good friends was not my fault. The biggest lie I have ever believed is that I was not enough, and it was my fault that people did not treat me kindly.

I viewed myself as unimportant. I didn't like what I saw in the mirror. How could I when all I felt was that I was not good enough? I didn't like my body because of comments that were made about it. I didn't like the way my eyes crinkled. I didn't like my heart and how it cared so much for others and was hurting all of the time. I didn't like myself because it felt like no one liked me. I know how it feels to want to scream in your pillow, or punch a hole in a wall, or to simply not want to exist anymore. I know the pain of losing friends, and of having friends make plans in front of you that you are not a part of. I know the pain of trying your best and always feeling like it is never enough; it is exhausting. Or thinking you can trust and count on an adult, only to have them let you down countless times, and make you feel like you aren't heard and don't matter.

Rejection tries to tell us why we are not good enough. Rejection tries to say that there is something wrong with us.

1. What I would forget to see are the expectations that set myself up to feel rejection. I knew how those girls treated each other, so it was unrealistic to expect them to treat me any differently.

2. I forgot to look at the person who is making me "feel" rejection. A lot of times rejection has way more to do with the person *doing* the rejecting than the person *being* rejected. It is not your fault. It is important to realize that everyone has choices. My birth dad made a choice to leave and chose to stay gone—without even really knowing me, proving that it wasn't my fault. Those girls not being good friends to me, but also not being very good friends to one another, proved that it wasn't my fault. They

are all hurt people, looking to hurt other people. Hurt people, hurt people.

3. I forgot to take responsibility for how I feel. Yep. You read that right. Water can only sink a ship if it gets inside the ship. Words can only hurt you or bring you down, if you believe they are true, or if you let them get to your heart. A lot of times I was the person who *allowed* myself to live in rejection. This does NOT mean that things won't hurt because they will, but maybe not as deep of a hurt. If you feel like you aren't good enough, and you believe that you aren't good enough, you better believe that you are going to act and allow yourself to be treated like you aren't good enough. What you think and say to yourself matters. At the end of the day, you decide who you are, how you are going to let people treat you, and who you want to be.

This feeling of being paralyzed, and not feeling happy does not have to last forever. The hurt you and I feel is temporary, but the lessons learned through it and the way it can grow us and make us who we were created to be, are forever. We are going to make it, you hear me? One day at a time. We will get through whatever storms this life has to throw at us, and we will be one step closer to the incredible people that we were created to be. You are going to change the world someday, and you don't even know it yet.

Ideas to remember from this section:

1. What do you reject about yourself?

_____

_____

_____

_____

_____

_____

_____

_____

2. How do you feel rejected by others?

_____

_____

_____

_____

_____

_____

_____

_____

Bela's Answers

1. Recently, I went swim suit shopping which makes me very anxious. I had a melt down after trying on over 20 swim suits because nothing fit right. I am learning to love and be comfortable in my body, but at the same time I reject parts of it.

2. I feel like people don't see me for who I really am. I want them to get to know my heart.

CHAPTER THREE
Feelings

> Feelings
> *Noun*
> *Plural noun:* **feelings**
> 1. an emotional state or reaction
> 2. a belief, especially a vague or irrational one.
> 3. a sensitivity to or intuitive understanding of.

One thing that has taken me a while to learn is that I don't have to follow my feelings. I can take steps to set myself up for success, instead of being all over the place because my feelings change every ten minutes. In this chapter, I will be talking to you about feelings and how I learned that they don't have to control my life.

When I was younger, I thought my feelings were the end all be all. If I felt a certain way, it MUST be true. Since I thought they were true that meant that I needed to listen and follow them. What I found when I did that was that:

1. My feelings were all over the place and constantly changing.

2. How I felt was not always the truth, but it was always valid.

3. No one can read my mind or know how I feel unless I tell them.

As a girl, and in particular a teenage girl, I tend to get moody and emotional. If you are anything like me, I am sure that you can relate to one moment feeling like crying and the next feeling like laughing. It is crazy. My feelings are constantly changing and are constantly all over the place. Following them is like going on a wild goose chase. If I acted on every single feeling that I have ever had I would be such a mess; my brain would be on the Hoarders show because it would be so messy.

For example, one day I was having a bad day, and I was already crabby. I was driving home, and I was pep talking myself. "Okay Bela, I know you're in a bad mood. Your family didn't cause this bad mood, so you shouldn't take it out on them. Calm down and be nice." Or something like that. I felt calm. I sat outside in my car and took a few deep breaths before walking inside.

I walked inside, and my mom instantly said, "What's wrong?" All of the anger and annoyance I had just pushed down came building back up, and I snapped "NOTHING" in a sassy tone that would for sure get me grounded or at least scowled at.

"Sure, *sounds* like nothing," was the response I got. I felt so much annoyance and rage that I had no reason to feel towards my mom.

My mom didn't do anything to me. She just happened to touch a sore spot without realizing it was there. I shouldn't have expected her to know I was having a bad day. I should have just told her right away "Hey mom, nothing is wrong. Really. I just had a bad day and am kind of in a bad mood." Boom. That would have helped so much. Instead, my brain was thinking thoughts like "See that? She's trying to make you angry. She knew you had a bad day and now she is trying to make it worse." As if my mother would sit and try to egg me on. But that's the thing — A lot of the time, my feelings lie to me. I feel like I am not good enough, I feel like I'm not pretty enough, I feel like I am weird or invisible, and I feel like people are trying to hurt me on purpose, etc. That isn't true. My brain is so smart it can trick me into believing lies. Here's the truth: *you are good enough, pretty enough, you aren't weird or invisible.*

Your feelings will run your life unless you take the time to be aware of how you are feeling. It is completely normal to feel ANY feeling. No feeling is bad. What is bad is letting a feeling dictate how you live, what you do, or how you feel about yourself. Emotions are normal but are not always right. You have feelings every day, so it is important to pay attention to how you deal with them and learn useful ways to deal with them.

There are healthy ways and unhealthy ways.

Unhealthy	Healthy
Gossip	Listen to music
Slander	Write
Self-harm	Talk about the feelings
Isolation	Exercise
Denial	Cry
Bullying	Punch a pillow
Substance Use	Take a bath/ relax

Honestly, one of the hardest things for me to do is to feel my feelings. It is so easy to numb out, distract myself, and push them away. I try to forget them or cover them up, so I don't have to deal with them. The problem with this is that my feelings are inside of me. So, no matter how far I run, or how much I try to forget, they will still be there. Distracting yourself will work for a while, but in the end, every unresolved or undealt with feeling will still be there in your heart.

What do you do with your feelings?

_____

_____

_____

_____

_____

_____

_____

_____

_____

_____

_____

_____

_____

_____

_____

_____

_____

I have gone to therapy since I was 5-years-old. So, about thirteen years now. My therapist is well aware that I tend to decide things base on how I feel. If I feel angry, I might act out in anger like sassing off to my parents or using some not-very-nice words. If I feel like I am left out, chances are I'll stop talking and withdrawal from the conversation, and act like I am left out. Sometimes I won't be able to even think straight, and I'll have irrational feelings. Irrational feelings are feelings that don't make sense or don't really go with the situation at hand. They are usually overwhelming and distracting. I might have so many feelings all at once that I have a hard time figuring out what is true and what isn't.

My therapist showed me something that has helped me so much, and I am going to share it with you.

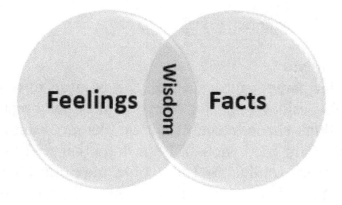

So first, when I am in a situation, I list off my feelings. For example: Imagine at school there is this girl whose parents just went through a divorce. For some reason, she is super mean to you. She always has something mean to say to or about you. She makes fun of how you talk, the way you walk, the clothes you wear, your hair, and your laugh. You feel like you can never get away from her and that everyone likes her more than they like you because she makes you look dumb.

You walk the halls everyday feelings not good enough, left out, ugly, and angry. You feel like you want to crawl under a rock and hide.

So, with this chart, you would write down the feelings you have been feeling.

Feelings:

Sad, angry, hopeless, helpless, not enough, ugly, left out, insecure, annoyed, dumb. Feel that you want to be mean back. Feel the need to switch schools. Can't handle it anymore.

Facts:

Her parents got a divorce. She is mean to other people besides you. Not everyone likes her because they think she is mean. People do like me. I am not dumb. I am good enough. I can find other friends to hang around. I like my laugh. I like the clothes that I wear. Sometimes my hair is annoying and messy, but I still like it. I shouldn't be mean back because that won't help, but I could ask her to stop.

After we list both the feelings and the facts, and we have a better, more rational perspective, we go back and look at both of them to decide what the truth is. In this example, the conclusion would look something like this:

This girl at school is mean. She makes me feel really angry, sad, and insecure about myself. I know her parents are going through a divorce so maybe she is having a hard time and taking it out on me. She hurts my feelings, and my feelings tell me that I'm not enough, but I am. My feelings tell me that I am dumb, but I am smart. My feelings tell me that I should be mean back to her, but I know that won't help anything. Maybe I should talk to my mom or the counselor, or maybe even to her to tell her how she is making me feel.

To be able to tell people how they make us feel, we first have to learn how to communicate our feelings. A lot of times people communicate through body language if something makes them uncomfortable. Some people self-harm as a cry for help. Some write to get all of their thoughts out. What a lot of people don't do, is talk to someone else about their feelings. This is super important because:

1. We tend to think that other people already know how we feel.

2. A lot tends to get jumbled in our brain and speaking out loud helps to sort through rational and irrational feelings.

It is essential to find someone who you trust to be able to talk to. Maybe it is an aunt, mom, counselor, or therapist. That way you don't have to worry about what you have to say getting shared with others, and you will feel more comfortable opening up. It is important to remember that nothing you feel is wrong or bad. There are NO bad feelings, and you shouldn't let anyone tell you how you can or can't feel. Your feelings are YOUR feelings. That being said, it is not helpful to let feelings consume you. This is why you talk to others about them.

Sometimes when I need to talk to someone about my feelings, I write out what I am going to say first. For example, let's look at the story I told you earlier when I snapped at my mom because I had a bad day. What if I had sat in my car and typed out, "hey mom, I have been having a really bad day, and I am not in a good mood. I am going to try my best not to have attitude" and then walked inside and told her that? I would have been prepared with what to say. This practice is so helpful.

I totally get it. It is really freaking scary to open up and tell someone how you are really feeling. You may be scared of getting judged or getting looked at differently. The only way to truly deal with your feelings is to be honest about them. You are the person who you tend to trick and lie to the most. Nothing gets healed by lying about it. Your words are powerful, and something in us gets set free when we speak the truth out loud: the truth about the hard time you are going through, the truth about your struggles with your appearance, the truth about how your "friends" make you feel.

We as a society have been brain-washed to think that if we have struggles or insecurities, then we are messed up. That is nowhere near the truth. Struggles, insecurities, hard times, feelings that won't go away, these are things which make us who we are. Our feelings do not define us; what we do with them does.

I have *a choice* in what I do with my feelings. I never knew this when I was younger, but I really wish that I had. Just because I *felt* angry did not mean that I had to *act* angry. Just because I felt sad did not mean I had to mope around. I could choose. Sure, I can allow my feelings to decide what I do, but if I do, I need to prepare to be all over the place.

I will say it a million times. Whatever feelings you are feeling are OKAY, but they are not always right.

Yep

Read that again. *Whatever feelings you are feeling are okay, but that does not mean that they are always right.* I emphasize this so much because your feelings are important. No one else in this world knows how you feel except you. You know when you feel uncomfortable. You know when something feels off. You know when you feel bothered and angry. You know when something feels light and joyful. The more you start to pay attention to your feelings the more you will be able to control them and change things in your life that aren't good for you.

Something that I do, when I am trying not to let my feelings rule my life, is recognize them and then change my perspective. For example: Imagine that girl at school is being really mean to you, but you are so sick of feeling upset and having bad days. I would take a deep breath and pause.

I would stop to think about how I am really feeling, and I would talk myself through it. "What am I feeling? Anger, sadness, annoyance? Okay, I feel angry. Okay. Feeling angry is okay, but I don't have to let my anger run my day. Instead, I am going to try to find little things to be happy about. Maybe I will even compliment a couple of people." That is somewhat what the thought pattern is for me.

Here is the thing: when you see everything through the lens of your feelings, you give them more power, and they feel stronger. But when you take time to mentally think through and validate how you are feeling, and then tell yourself you are going to choose to look at things differently, it strips our feelings of their control. They won't go away, but by choosing to look at things outside of your feelings will keep them from being as strong and present.

When you look for something, you will always see it. For example, if I go to school every day and look for anything negative or bad, I will find it, because it is always there. But if I go to school and decide I will look for all of the good, positive, happy stuff - I will find it instead, because it is also always there. The difference lies in what you are looking for, and that is your choice. You get to choose whether you are going to let your feelings push you to look for the bad, or if you are going to look for the good. I promise you, every day in life, both the good and the bad will be there. The one you see most is the one that you choose to see.

Sometimes when I go through a really tough time, it almost feels impossible to find anything good. I have lain in bed crying because I could not think of a single good thing about the situation I was in. I have felt so hopeless and sad. I've had people tell me that whatever happened, happened for a reason, and it will all be okay. I have wanted to scream at those people. I did NOT feel like it was going to be okay. Just because it was for a reason did not make it hurt any less or make it any easier to go through.

I learned that when my feelings are hurt, I get a wound. I like to compare this to a cut on the skin. When I get a cut on my skin, it hurts like heck, bleeds, scabs, and sometimes scars. When I get hurt, my heart needs time to hurt (or bleed). What I have found is it is OKAY to be hurting. If something happens to you that hurts your feelings that is perfectly normal. You have to let your heart bleed in order for it to scab. If you just try to ignore it and distract yourself from it - the hurt will still be there, bleeding, and taking longer to heal. After time has passed, the wound still hurts, but not as much as it did at first. This is usually when the scab has formed.

Can you remember a time where you had a cut, and you accidentally bumped, scraped, or hit it, and it busted open? It started hurting pretty bad again and bled again, didn't it? When your hurt starts to heal, if you keep poking at it, picking at it, and thinking about it, you reopen the hurt, and it takes longer to heal.

After a little while, it will scab again, and possibly even scar. The scar will remind you how much it hurt. Just like scars fade, the hurt may lessen, but the memories will always remain. They serve as a reminder that if you can get through that hurt, you can get through the hurts that may follow. You may have the opportunity to show people your scars and use them to help others through their healing. Your struggles may serve as an encouragement for someone else to keep fighting their own battle.

My point in all of this is, to heal you have to let it hurt, let it bleed, and let it go. You have to stop pouring salt in your wounds and poking them. You have to stop touching your wounds in order for them to heal. I am just as guilty of this as anyone. I might find myself looking at old photos to make myself sad, watching sad movies, or listening to sad music. Pretty much forcing myself to be sad and to relive the hurt. Other times, I put pressure on myself to "be okay" right away, when that is so unrealistic. We cannot expect ourselves to just get over having our feelings hurt. It is a process from the inside out, just like the healing of a cut. So next time you want to cry because something is STILL bothering you, remember that it is part of the healing, and it takes time. Remember that cuts don't heal in a day. Don't be so hard on yourself, because that won't change anything.

I thought all my life that if I felt sad, then people wouldn't like me, and I would be a burden. I didn't think that I was worth as much when I was sad, compared to when I was happy. I always pretended to be happy and have a smile on my face no matter what - even if on the inside I was crying. I hid my feelings and acted like I was okay because I desperately just wanted to *be* okay. I ignored my feelings and problems because I thought they would go away. The only way to deal with your pain is to go through it. Running from the hurt feelings, and the wounds won't do any good because they are within you. That's why we heal from the inside out – similar to a cut.

I did not do a very good job of truly letting myself acknowledge and feel my feelings when I got hurt. I liked to act like I was okay. I never wanted anyone to see me hurt. One day, I exploded – all of the feelings I was holding inside burst out of me. Tears would not stop streaming down my face. I had a lump in my throat, and I felt like screaming. My mother didn't know what hit me or what happened. She looked at me as if I had just gotten news that someone had died. She had no idea about all the hurt I was feeling. She didn't know that I would cry myself to sleep some nights. She didn't know that under all of my smiles was pain because I hid it. She looked so surprised, and she was sad that I hadn't talked to someone, anyone about how I was feeling. I didn't know how, and I didn't want everyone to know how much I was struggling.

Struggling or not being able to recognize or control your feelings does not mean something is wrong with you. I have been there, and I had no idea how to even begin to recognize my feelings or tell someone how I was feeling. It is something we have to learn and practice each day. You need to practice saying to that girl who said something mean, "Hey I don't like when you talk to me like that." Or when you are feeling sad, learn to share these feelings with someone. Or even when you are having a good day, practice sharing your happy feelings with someone. You get to make a choice each day, maybe even each hour. You need to remind yourself that you have a choice.

All of this is important because you will have feelings every day for the rest of your life. Learning how to recognize the feelings you have, control them, and communicate them or do something about them is vital. It does not happen overnight, and that is okay. Learning to love yourself no matter what you are feeling is important because your feelings do not change who you are, and they do not determine your worth. Hour by hour, the more you do it, the easier it will be.

Ideas to remember from this chapter:

1. What feelings most consume you?

_____

_____

_____

_____

_____

_____

_____

2. What ways do you deal with your feelings?
    (Remember the chart above, use if needed)

_____

_____

_____

_____

_____

_____

_____

_____

3. Is there anything that you can do better or change about how you deal with your feelings?

_____

_____

_____

_____

_____

_____

_____

_____

4. Write three things that you are thankful for:

1. _____

2. _____

3. _____

Bela's Answers

1. The feelings that most consume me are rejection, not being good enough, anxiety, and feeling overwhelmed.

2. I deal with my feelings in many different ways depending on what I need that day.
   I like to:
   • Journal   • drive & listen to music   • Exercise

3. Sometimes I get scared of feeling my feelings so I push them down and ignore them. I can be better at giving myself permission to feel my feelings, instead of ignoring them.

4. 1. My family
   1. Coffee
   3. Journaling

CHAPTER FOUR

Self-Talk

Self-Talk
Noun
1. the act or practice of talking to oneself, either aloud or silently.
Self-talk is the way you talk to yourself. It is your inner voice.

You may not even realize that you are constantly talking to yourself, but you are. Self-talk is critical because it is the voice you hear nonstop and most importantly, it is your voice. What you say to yourself and what you think about yourself affects how you live your everyday life.

Take a second before continuing on to answer these questions. Please be totally honest; there are no wrong or bad answers. It is super important to be honest with yourself and aware of where you are, so you know the things you need to work on.

Here they are!!!:

1. What do you do with what other people say about you?

   _____

   _____

   _____

   _____

   _____

2. How do you talk to yourself?

   _____

   _____

   _____

   _____

   _____

3. What do you think about yourself?

_____

_____

_____

_____

_____

Imagine waking up every day and having a person regularly whispering in your ear, telling you that you're not good enough. Imagine they tell you, "You look fat in that shirt," or "You should be more like that girl." What if the voice says that you should just be quiet because what you think doesn't matter anyway and the voice compares to anyone it can? Imagine that voice judges others too. It can't help but to tear others down and, in the process, tears you down with them. This voice criticizes every little thing you do. How would you feel constantly having this voice in your head? Never ending?

Well, you *would* probably feel like you look fat in that shirt, you *would* wish you were more like her, you *wouldn't* speak up, and you *would* constantly compare yourself to and judge others. You would be stuck in a cycle of negativity and insecurity.

Guess what? Most of us are.

You're not alone. You don't need someone else to whisper all of these things in your ears when you are already saying all of these things to yourself. I think the fact that it is your own self tearing you down is what hurts the most because if you aren't good enough for yourself, who are you good enough for? If you don't love yourself or see value in who you are, why would anyone else? There is value in you, even when you do not see it.

This is why self-talk is SO important. The way you speak to yourself has so much power. It will affect every single thing that you do, from the way you dress to the way you handle relationships. Your self-talk affects how you treat others and let them treat you. It plays a huge role in all of your relationships. How you treat people is a direct reflection of how you treat yourself and think about yourself.

We often emphasize what other people think about us, and not what we think about ourselves. I think that needs to change. At the end of the day, when you lay your head down at night, you have to be able to live with who you are. Only *you* have control over who you are and who you become.

Your self-talk goes hand in hand with your feelings. You feel emotions every hour of every day. But what a lot of people do not realize is that you have the power to decide how much you are going to allow the feelings to affect you. You do this with self-talk. With each feeling that you feel, you have a choice whether you are going to sit in it and let it ruin your mood, and possibly your day, OR to feel the feeling and not allow it to control you.

How you talk to yourself about how you are feeling is important. These are YOUR feelings after all. Thoughts like these are toxic, and you should try to pay attention and catch yourself when you start to think them:

- I shouldn't feel like this.
- Something must be wrong with me.
- This shouldn't bother me.
- I am so stupid.

- I need to be tougher.
- I don't want anyone to know this is how I feel.
- This is why no one likes me.
- I am such a mess.
- This feeling will never go away.

The words *would*, *could*, and *should* are words of shame. Nothing good comes with those words ever. These thoughts are toxic because either you do, or you don't. "I shouldn't feel like this" is a toxic thought because you do feel that way and telling yourself you shouldn't makes you feel ashamed. It turns you against yourself. There is absolutely nothing wrong with any feeling that you could possibly have in your life. People will tell you that feeling angry is bad, or feeling insecure is bad, or feeling "not enough" is bad. When they say these things all they are doing is avoiding the way they are feeling. Feelings are JUST feelings. They don't mean anything. Some may feel less pleasant than others, but it is such a great gift that we are able to feel at all. Instead of telling yourself thoughts like the ones above, realize how you feel and tell yourself that it is okay that you feel like that. That way you won't be in a constant battle with yourself, and you will be able to be more of who you truly are.

When you become more of who you truly are, what people think or say about you won't affect or bother you as much because you are focusing more on what you think of yourself. Can you imagine loving yourself so much that nothing that anyone says could tear you down? It would still hurt your feelings, but it wouldn't make you question yourself. You could feel hurt but brush it off your shoulders and remind yourself who you are. You could wake up every day and look in the mirror and love what you see regardless of what other people say. Doesn't that sound like a dream?

Guess what? You can live like that. You can live in such a way that the words that come out of other people's mouths do not change how you feel about yourself. I remember when I was in eighth grade when I felt down about myself or life, I would google positive quotes. I swear I changed my phone background like twice a week, but this is something I really liked to do. I remember one day, I was sitting on the couch with my feet on the footrest. I was wearing jeans and a blue Aéropostale shirt, with my hair in a messy bun. I was scrolling through google when I saw it:

"An entire sea of water cannot sink a ship unless it gets inside the ship. Similarly, the negativity of the world can't put you down unless you allow it to get inside of you."

– Goi Nasu

I sat there stunned and read it three more times. That's the very first time that I realized that all the bad things people say about me or to me, do not have to affect me. I one-hundred-percent know that it does not stop what they say from hurting, I just know that I have a choice in how much I am going to let it hurt. Are you going to sit and replay what they said over and over and over until it drives you nuts? Are you going to let someone's words make you doubt or dislike yourself? Are you going to give them the power to ruin your mood or day?

Or are you going to let it sting for a hot second and remind yourself who you are? Remind yourself what you love about yourself. Remind yourself things that you are thankful for. Maybe even think something positive about the person who was mean to you. Being negative takes just as much energy as being positive; the choice is up to you which one you would rather be. It is a minute-by-minute choice; it does not just happen. The more you choose, the easier it will be to choose again. So, if you choose to be negative all the time, it is going to be really easy to be negative, and same with being positive.

Affirmations were a really big game changer for my self-talk when I notice myself getting negative or insecure. Sometimes I will take time to write them out, other times I will just say them to myself. I have a list of them that I wrote, and I taped to my wall.

Here are some that are on my list:

I am enough.	I am strong.
I am loved.	I am in control of my thoughts.
I am beautiful.	I am choosing to be positive.
I am brave.	I am kind.
I am important.	I am changing the world.

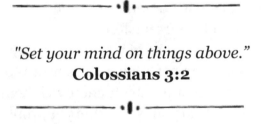

"Set your mind on things above."
Colossians 3:2

No matter what anyone has to say to me or about me, nothing will ever change those affirmations. Maybe I won't feel like they are true, but in the last chapter we talked about how our feelings are not always true. So, the next time someone speaks negatively to you, remind yourself who you are. Do not be defined by the words of others, because they are just words.

I promised you that I would be as real and honest as I can be. The problem is not what other people say to you, or about you. The problem is what you say to yourself, about yourself. Girl, I get it. Life is really hard, and it knocks you down a lot. Life and other people will push you down enough. You don't need to push your-self down with them. You need to be your own biggest fan, and this starts with how you talk to yourself.

If you had a friend, who spoke the way you speak to yourself would you keep that friend around? Would you allow them to speak to you that way? Would you ever say what you say to yourself to one of your friends? If you are being honest, the answer is, "Heck no!" You would not. I am right there with you. I am super critical of myself, and honestly not very nice to myself a lot of the time. I used to spend all of my time trying to get approval from everyone around me. I would do whatever I could to please them and to avoid making them angry at me. I would bend over backward for people who aren't even flexible themselves. I didn't care because I so desperately wanted someone to tell me how loved I was, how enough I was, how much I mattered. I wanted someone to speak life into me. I searched and searched, and each time I didn't get what I was looking for. It only made me want approval more. I wanted approval so much that I started changing how I acted, the way I dressed, who I would hang out with. I basically changed who I was just so I would be accepted. How often do you do this? Frantically change things about your beautiful self just to be told you are still enough.

I learned the harsh truth. The person I need acceptance from the most is me. The person who needs to tell me how wonderful, loved, and enough I am is myself. Until you accept yourself and speak love to yourself, no one else will, because you teach people how to treat you. This starts the second you wake up every day. It's the thoughts you have when you look in the mirror, when you've messed up, when you feel sad, and when you are comparing. You have the power every second of every single day to remind yourself how wonderful, loved, and enough you are.

Maybe just like me, you get so caught up in what you don't like about yourself, or what you wish that you could change that you forget to take time to look at the things that you love about yourself. We think if we hate ourselves that maybe things will change. Maybe if we hate ourselves enough, we will become skinny. Maybe if we hate ourselves enough, others will like us. Maybe if we hate ourselves enough, we will become good enough. Does that make any sense to you? If I hate myself enough, maybe I will start to love myself?

In this day in age, we focus so much on hate. Hate destroys. Hate does not help us grow. Hate does not change anything for the better. You cannot hate yourself better. You cannot hate yourself skinny. You cannot hate yourself prettier. You cannot hate yourself to love more. Only love can do that. You can love yourself to be more positive. You can love yourself to take care of yourself and so that you become skinnier. You can love the face looking back at you in the mirror and realize how pretty you have been this entire time. Hate blinds, love heals.

Do you want to be around people who are regularly tearing themselves down? Maybe that is why you don't like yourself. I know this is hard to hear and may seem harsh. I promised you that I would be nothing but honest and real with you. This is the truth, and this is important for you to hear, for your soul and for how you choose to live the rest of your life. I wish someone would have sat me down and told me all of this when I was younger. I wish I would have known that I didn't have to be so stinking mean to myself. I don't have to like everything about myself, but I don't have to tear the parts that I don't like down. This is so important, and I do not want you to miss this. You cannot treat someone better than the way you talk about them. This includes yourself. I will say that again: *You cannot treat someone better than the way you talk about them.*

Ideas to remember from this chapter:

1. What are three common thoughts you have about yourself?

   1. _____

   2. _____

   3. _____

2. Make an affirmations list. (See mine for example)

   _____

   _____

   _____

   _____

   _____

   _____

   _____

   _____

   _____

   _____

   _____

3. What is one thing that you can do today to show love
to yourself?

_____

_____

_____

_____

_____

_____

_____

_____

Bela's Answers

1. • I'm not doing enough.
   • I want to like myself more.
   • I am going to be okay.

2. I am enough.
   I am strong.
   I am loved.
   I am important.

3. One thing I can do to show love to myself is to try to think more positive. Im going to try and pay more attention to what I am saying to myself, and do my best to be nicer to myself.

CHAPTER FIVE

Identity

> Identity
> *noun*
> 1. the condition of being oneself.
> 2. who a person or what a thing is; the qualities, beliefs
> , etc., that distinguish a person or thing.

There are many different places you can find your identity or place your identity in without realizing you are doing so. Some examples are sports, boys, girls, friends, car, approval, grades, art, social media, etc.

For the longest time, I found my identity in sports. I played basketball and volleyball for nine years and five of those years had me playing both sports, year-round. That was all I did with my time, and I strove for approval in both of them. I was super hard on myself and mean to myself. Nothing I ever did was good enough. I compared my skills to others instead of trying to be the best I could be. If I messed up, I would beat myself up instead of just shaking it off and trying to do better next time.

It got to be so bad that my volleyball coach benched me until I started to be nicer to myself. He told me "you're killing yourself." He said that he wouldn't play me until I could figure out to stop being so critical and mean to myself. I honestly didn't realize that what I was doing was that bad, because it was normal to me.

I slowly started not to like sports as much. I kept thinking to myself that there had to be more to life than sports. All I ever did was sports. My dislike grew, and I decided that sports weren't filling me up. I didn't want to give them all of my time anymore. I had a conversation with each of my coaches, and I quit.

I didn't realize that not playing would affect me as much as it did. It felt like part of me was gone. I was depressed for a while and did not know what to do with my newfound free time. It was tough to let that big piece of my life go, because part of who I was, was rooted in it. I wanted to grow as a person and become stronger in my identity. What I didn't know is that every single person I have ever met is part of my identity. They all have played some sort of role in making me who I am today. Some roles are obviously way bigger than others. The people you spend the most time with have the most significant impact on who you are. It is the company you keep.

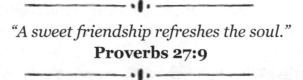

"A sweet friendship refreshes the soul."
Proverbs 27:9

You become who you hang out with. Bad company corrupts good character. If your best friend is negative and doesn't make very good decisions, chances are this negativity and poor decision-making will rub off on you. It is crucial to surround yourself with people who you want to be like. Your five closest friends are who you are destined to be like. Knowing this makes it okay to be super picky about who you spend time with. If someone weighs you down, it is okay not to spend as much time with them.

Your identity is also found in what you do to fill yourself up. No, I am not talking about food. I am talking about food for your soul. What activities do you do to help your heart and mind? What do you do to fill yourself? Do you hang out with friends, watch TV, read, draw, talk to people, etc.? It is important that we spend time doing things that are aligned with who we want to be. The books you read will play a part in your identity; they are soul food. The music you listen to will impact how you see others and yourself. It will be part of your identity since it is filling your brain. The TV shows you watch will also impact you. You may pick up sayings, mannerisms, or ideas from TV that will influence who you are.

Without realizing it, you can put anything into your identity. Our identity is found where you spend most of your time. It is kind of scary to think that you could put searching for someone's love or approval into your identity. What happens when they don't give it to you? What happens when they are not there anymore? One person can make such a massive impact on your life. It is essential to find your identity in yourself and in the one who created you. Otherwise, you will always be searching for something to make your life feel worthwhile.

My sense of identity affects everything I do. It affects how I talk to myself, how I handle situations, how I view myself, and the choices I make. Everything. Who you are matters. What you do matters. Who you want to be matters. This is the only life that you get. I want you to spend it being who you truly are, not who everyone thinks you should be. I want your heart to sing and be full of joy because you say "yes" to what helps you, and "no" to what hurts you.

I know how it feels to try to figure out who you are and why you are here. Maybe you feel like you shouldn't be here. I have felt that too.

If you have breath in your lungs, you have a purpose on this earth. God doesn't just make people and leave them. He makes them for a reason, and he has big plans for you. He already adores who you are. I know it feels like you need to be someone else, or you need to be better than who you are. And you will be. But remember to love yourself where you are right now. You've been working hard to be this person too. She deserves some love.

Please don't get so caught up in who you should be that you miss who you are. Who you are right now is already pretty stinking wonderful. You will grow, you will learn, you will get better, and you will get there. One day at a time. All you can do right now, today, is your best. Do your best today and do your best tomorrow.

Spend more time doing things that make your heart happy. Dance around your room in your underwear, tell jokes, watch funny videos, watch the sunset, and write letters to people who you love, or write a letter to yourself telling yourself how awesome you are.

There is nothing in this world that can make you unlovable.

- You are so loved.
- You are so worthy.
- You are enough.
- Your heart will heal.
- You will be okay.
- You will get through this.
- I am right there along-side you.
- I have been there.
- The world needs what you have to offer.
- This world is only ever going to get one *you*. Be *you* with your whole heart, babe.

———————— •❘• ————————

"If you hit a wall, climb over it, crawl under it, or dance on top of it."
- Unknown

———————— •❘• ————————

Ideas to remember from this chapter:

1. What are qualities that you have that you like?

_____

_____

_____

_____

_____

_____

_____

2. What are qualities you want to improve?

_____

_____

_____

_____

_____

_____

_____

3. What are things you do to fill yourself up?

_____

_____

_____

_____

_____

_____

_____

4. What are some of your favorite books, shows, and songs?

_____

_____

_____

_____

_____

_____

_____

5. Where do you find your identity?

_____

_____

_____

_____

_____

_____

_____

_____

Bela's Answers

1. Some qualities that I like are:
   - My love for people
   - My humor
   - My honesty
   - My boldness

2. I want to get better at:
   - Being paitent
   - Being positive
   - Being confident
   - Being consistent

3. Things I do to fill myself up:
   - Read the Bible • Journal • Spend time with family
   - pray • Jam • Church, Youth group.

4. Favorite Books:
   - The Giver by Lois Lowry
   - Uninvited by Lysa Terkeurst
   - The Selection by Kiera Cass
   - Girl, Stop apologizing by Rachel Hollis

   Favorite Shows:
   - Spongebob
   - Family Feud
   - One tree hill
   - Saved by the Bell

   Favorite Songs:
   - Steady Me by Hollyn ft. Aaron Cole
   - Everything's magic by Angels & Airwaves
   - Rise up by Andra Day
   - One Thing by Finger Eleven

   I'm such a music junkie, it was hard
   to choose.

5. Growing up, without realizing I found my identity in sports. Now I am doing my best to find my identity in the one who created me. I still catch myself searching for my identity in others approval and what they think. I have to remind myself who God says I am. It's a daily struggle, but I'm doing my best.

CHAPTER SIX

Comparison

> Comparison
> *noun*
> 1. the process of tearing yourself down or building yourself up based upon differences or similarities between yourself and another person or thing.

Have you ever walked through the mall and shopped off of other people? No, I am not talking about walking up to someone and trying to buy the shirt they are wearing. I am talking about comparing yourself to the people you see.

Maybe your thoughts were something like "Man, I wish I had her legs," "Wow, why can't I look like her?" "I don't like her, she's so skinny," "I wish my butt were that nice," "I am so much prettier than her," or "What in the world is she wearing?" It is as if we walk around acting like what we have or look like is never as good as what someone else has or looks like. We always want what other people have, or we tear others down to make ourselves feel better and in the process, and we tell ourselves that who we are and what we have isn't good enough.

This is partly why comparison hurts you so much. You are ingraining in your head that you will never be as good as other people AND that you don't like yourself. People who like themselves do not need to compare. Comparing ourselves is never about being happy for the other person. It is usually fueled by anger and insecurity. We feel like our looks aren't good enough, and so we compare. We shop for what we want instead of loving what we already have. As if our shopping off of other girls is going to make us who we want to be. It also might happen that the quality you love about another person, might be the very thing they hate about themselves.

It is so easy to compare everything and anything. We compare our looks, our friends, our hurts, our accomplishments, our families, our social media pages, our cars, our pets, our houses, and so much more. If that isn't enough, we now have technology in our hands 24/7 that actually makes comparison easier than it already was. Now instead of waiting to see Stacey in school tomorrow to compare yourself to her, you can go on all of her social media pages to criticize and compare nonstop. While you compare yourself to her or anyone else, all you are doing is giving yourself reasons why you are not good enough. And we wonder why so many people feel as if they are not good enough, comparison is one of the biggest reasons.

I was there. I remember being in middle school and comparison was like its own language. It was as if, if you weren't comparing yourself, then you weren't cool. It was uncool to be okay with who you are, which makes no sense, because deep down inside of every person, is someone who just wants to be loved and be themselves.

It was as if the people who were being themselves were "weird" because, in middle school, not a lot of people like themselves yet. Middle school is the time to start figuring out who you are and who you want to be. It was intimidating when other people liked themselves enough to be who they are, instead of to just fit in. It also caused people to be insecure and jealous of those who did know who they wanted to be.

Comparison is the death of contentment. Comparison will kill anything that you like about yourself, or your life. It will make you take things for granted. It will make you question everything, and you will never be satisfied. You will always compare to make yourself feel better, maybe if you compare your life to someone else's yours doesn't seem as bad. But in the end, all you are doing is running away from the feelings of insecurity and judgment you feel towards yourself.

Comparison is the thief of joy. Instead of enjoying your peaceful time at the beach, for example, you might sit and compare your body with everyone around you. This will cause insecurity and steal the joy of your day. You will never be happy with anything you have or are doing because comparison will make it seem like what you have is not that good. When you compare, you rob yourself of being joyful because you are focusing on everything you are *not*, instead of everything that you *are*.

Comparison is so hurtful because you were made to be *you*, not them. You were made who you are for a reason. How sad would it be, to never be who you were created to be, all because you're too busy trying to be someone else? We are all unique. We all have differences, talents, and insecurities. Comparing ourselves doesn't change any of that. Comparing yourself does not make you any better, smarter, prettier, happier, or healthier. All it does is make you insecure and steal your joy.

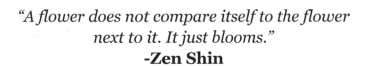

"A flower does not compare itself to the flower next to it. It just blooms."
-Zen Shin

I bloomed a little bit faster than many of the girls in my grade. By bloom, I mean I got boobs first. At the time I wasn't aware of it, but this caused a lot of comparison.

It happened while I was walking through the crowded hallway full of teenagers and pre-teens laughing out loud, glaring, and gossiping. On my way to class, a girl named Britney approached me. Wearing yoga pants and grinning, she asked me if I had gotten a boob job. Yep, you read that right. When I was thirteen years old, in seventh grade, I got asked if I had gotten a boob job. When I heard her question, I thought it was so ridiculous that I laughed and told her, "No."

I thought it was a random question, but it turns out that she wasn't the only one wondering, she was just the only one with enough courage to ask. It felt like the whole school thought I had gotten a boob job. Turns out, that an eighth-grader started the rumor, and her older sister joined in, which made the rumor also spread to the high schoolers. From that day on, I would get comments all over my Instagram posts, and to make things worse, random people would snicker and laugh in the halls. I wanted to crawl in a hole.

I started consciously wearing baggy clothes, but I still cried almost every day after school. I felt ashamed of my body, and I tried to hide how I looked. It was something I had no control over. My boobs were simply there. I could feel myself and those around me dripping in comparison. Girls wanted to have boobs like me, and well, to be honest with you, I wanted boobs like them. I had thoughts like, "if I looked like that, this rumor would have never started," "I wish I looked like her," or "I wish I could wear shirts like that without feeling insecure." It was really hard for me to like who I was, and how I looked. Comparison became a habit of mine, and I became super unhappy and negative.

I not only compared myself at school but at home too. I would compare myself to my siblings. I thought that some of them were loved more than I was. I thought maybe I wasn't a good enough daughter. This affected my relationships with all of them because instead of wanting what was best for them, I wanted them to get in trouble so that I could look better.

I would compare myself with all of the girls around me and on social media. This caused me to become more insecure and mean to myself. I shared earlier that I was already negative and mean, but comparison did not help my self-talk at all. It made it one-hundred-percent worse.

Drastic events like a rumor do not need to happen in order for you to start comparing yourself to others. This was just a significant moment that I remember drowning in comparison. I believe comparison happens much more often and more "casually" than we think. I think it happens every time we go on social media, watch TV, go to prom, or go out with friends. It happens everywhere.

I slowly learned ways that I could catch myself when I was comparing. I learned how to flip my mindset. I still struggle with comparison. Now I do it much less frequently, and I catch myself more often. The very first thing that I ever did that helped me with my battle with comparison was to start to compliment people.

It started after the whole boob job incident. I was super negative, and I would cry a lot. I talked to my mom about what was going on. She challenged me to compliment three people every day at school, and truly mean the compliments. I didn't realize at the time, but now each day when I went to school, I started to look for the things that I liked about people so that I could tell them. This took some of my focus off of comparing and put it onto complimenting.

"Gracious words are like honeycombs, sweetness to the soul and health to the body."
Proverbs 16:24

It was a little uncomfortable at first, but once I continued to do it, I became a little more positive. Seeing people's faces light up when they received a compliment made me want to compliment more. It also helped me become better at receiving compliments, which can be uncomfortable. When I started to give compliments and receive them, I felt happier because I wasn't as worn out and torn down from comparison. I wasn't tearing myself down as much because instead of envying others, I was celebrating the beauty that they had, which in turn made me celebrate my own.

Another thing that helped me was affirmations. I know we have talked about them before, but they are so useful and crucial. What you think and say to yourself is everything. If you can catch yourself comparing and instead remind yourself who you are with an affirmation, it is a total game changer. Writing them down or even just reciting them to yourself makes a huge difference.

"A soft answer turns away wrath, but a harsh word stirs up anger."
Proverbs 15:1

One of the places I struggled with comparison the most was on social media. Everyone on social media posts their best life. So, when you are having a bad day, scrolling through social media, only seeing people's best days, messes with your head. It almost creates a false reality of how other people's lives really are, therefore holding unrealistic expectations for how your life should be.

What a lot of people won't show on their social medias are their bad days, bad selfies, arguments, insecurities, and other things they are struggling with. That does not mean that they are not struggling, because they are.

We don't usually get to see the insecurities and struggles that others have and a lot of the time we are comparing ourselves to a falsely painted picture of perfection. I find it so easy to open the app and compare myself to others, to their selfies, to their bodies, and to their lives. Social media can be a big confidence killer for me.

Sometimes I do this thing where I creep on people's profiles, and without realizing it, I compare the crap out of myself. I either tear that person down or tear myself down for not being like them. Every time, I was on social media I felt drained and insecure. I did not like feeling like that, so I chose to do a couple of things to help lessen the negative impact I was letting social media have on me.

1. I went through all of the people I followed, and I unfollowed people who I compared myself too, who posted inappropriate posts, who I didn't know, and the accounts that were hurting me more than helping me. To be honest with you, I think I unfollowed about five hundred accounts. I did not do this to be mean or to make anyone feel bad. I chose to do this to protect my heart. It is social media, and *you have control over who you follow and who you don't follow.*

2. After I unfollowed the negative accounts, I started the search for positive, inspirational accounts. I found some quote accounts, encourageing people doing amazing things, and accounts that were inspiring. Now, when I am on social media, I am filling my brain with inspiration, encouragement, and motivation, instead of, insecurity, comparison, and judgment.

3. Next, I started to pay more attention and tried to catch myself, when I started to compare myself to or judge someone else. Instead of letting myself continue to judge or compare I

would instead compliment them or affirm myself. Sometimes I got a little crazy with it and commented on their picture, genuinely complimenting them. When you compliment or celebrate someone, you have less room in your heart for comparison and envy. You also lift that person up.

After I unfollowed people, some of them made a big deal out of it and asked me why I didn't like them. I told them that it wasn't that I didn't like them. It was that what they were posting didn't serve me. I told them I was sorry it hurt their feelings and then I moved on. I knew that this was what was for the best, and it made my social media experience more positive. Just because someone doesn't like what you are doing, does not mean what you are doing is wrong. It is one-hundred-percent okay for you to unfollow people whose posts hurt your heart. *Your heart is more important than an Instagram post.*

The thing about us humans is that we like to compare because we are all different. We all have different qualities, talents, and skills if we all had the same skills the world would be a pretty boring place. Just because someone else has a quality, skill, or talent that you do not have does not make them better than you. Yes, maybe they can play the piano better than you can, or maybe they are super smart at math, and you're not, maybe you love sports, and they don't. That is what makes them unique. Their talents aren't the same as yours, and your talents aren't the same as theirs, but your worth is the same. We are all humans in this world, and we were made for love. No human, not even the president or a movie star, is better than any other human. We all just have different talents, skills, and qualities. Despite our differences and uniqueness, we are all loved the same.

Comparison is something we need to fight minute-by-minute. When we choose to compliment others, affirm ourselves, and protect our hearts, we will love ourselves more and compare ourselves less. All comparison does is show you your own insecurities. Instead, pretty girl, let's show love to our insecurities. Let's tell other girls things we like about them, and let's tell ourselves things we like about ourselves. Your self-talk is so important to overcome comparison. Once you compare less and compliment more, you will feel more joy and be more content with who you are and what you have. You are exactly who you are supposed to be, and you look exactly how you are supposed to. You were handpicked and crafted to be who you are. You are loved, beautiful, and enough. Please remember that putting out someone else's light does not make yours shine any brighter.

Ideas to remember from this chapter:

1. Where does comparison show up in your life?

_____

_____

_____

_____

_____

_____

_____

_____

2. Write five affirmations.

1. _____

2. _____

3. _____

4. _____

5. _____

3. Unfollow at least five people on social media whose accounts do not serve you (this includes Instagram, twitter, snapchat, Facebook, etc.).

4. Going forward, give three compliments each day and truly mean them.

Bela's Answers

1. I tend to compare myself with what I "should" be doing, or who I "should" be, instead of being okay with where I am in life. Comparison also shows up on social media a lot, so I try to be cautious of who I follow.

2.
- I am enough.
- I am exactly where I'm supposed to be.
- I am kind.
- What I have to say matters.
- I am loved.

CHAPTER SEVEN
Bullying

> Bullying
> *noun*
> 1. abuse and mistreatment of someone vulnerable by someone stronger, more powerful, etc.

Bullying is unwanted, aggressive, vindictive behavior that usually is repetitive. The bully is usually bigger, more popular, stronger, or has something over the target. There also can be multiple bullies. There are three different types of bullying.

1. Verbal bullying: saying or writing mean things.
   - Teasing
   - Name calling
   - Inappropriate sexual comments
   - Taunting
   - Threatening to cause harm

2. Social bullying: hurting someone's reputation or relationships.
   - Leaving someone out on purpose
   - Telling other people not to be friends with someone

- Spreading rumors
- Embarrassing someone in public

3. Physical bullying: hurting someone's body or possessions
   - Hitting/kicking/pinching
   - Spitting
   - Tripping/pushing
   - Taking or breaking someone's things
   - Making rude or mean hand gestures

Every person that I know has experienced some sort of bullying. Some even have been the bullies themselves. Surprisingly, before someone becomes a bully it is most likely that they have been bullied themselves. I personally have been bullied and have had everything I listed above happened to me except two things. Being bullied has taught me many different things.

I told you earlier that the friend group that I was a part of for some of my years in school was the "popular" clique. The one where all the girls are nice to your face—but talk about you behind your back. The clique that liked to make fun of others who weren't in the group or were "different" than them. Throughout my middle school, I was bullied by them, some members more than others.

One of the very first disputes between my friend group and me happened in sixth grade. One day, I was walking with Jane, my basketball teammate, to her dad's classroom to get the balls for practice. Her dad was one of our teachers and also our coach. Back in 2012, there was a popular belief going around that the world was going to end in the middle of December. So, naturally, this was a topic that everyone was talking about at school. As we were going to get the basketballs, she asked me what I believed happened after we die. I told her that I think that you have to ask Jesus into your heart and have a relationship with Jesus to go to heaven. I believed that baptism was a way of *showing* everyone that you have a relationship with Him, not the way to get to heaven. She raised her eyebrows silently and nodded. She didn't say anything in return. I knew that she and I had grown up differently and that we didn't believe the same things, but at the time I didn't think anything more about it.

A few weeks later, I was at her house. We were hanging out and playing games on the computer. I asked her if I was staying over or going home, and she didn't answer. Instead, she walked away while I sat at her dining room table watching SpongeBob and eating fruit loops. I sat there for what felt like forever. I was so anxious, wondering if she was okay, or if she didn't want to be my friend anymore, or if I had done something wrong.

When she came back, I could see the tear stains around her eyes. I was super confused. No one stopped to tell me what was going on. Her dad simply told me I had to go home, so he drove me home. In the car, he didn't say a word to me. All I could think of was, "What the heck happened? What was wrong with Jane? Did I do something? Were we still friends?"

Later, my parents got a phone call saying that her dad was going to come over and talk to them. They sat me down and told me to tell them if something bad had happened, so they weren't caught off guard. I said "No," that I couldn't think of anything. Her dad came over, and they talked. He told them that I was too bold and that I always pick on the weaker kids. He then told my parents that Jane had been crying at night and having nightmares because she was scared that she was going to hell. He also told my parents that *I* told her that she was going to hell and that I was not allowed at their house anymore.

After he left, my parents filled me in. I was shocked and upset. I cried because I didn't want to lose a friend and I was upset that she lied. She had just asked me what I believed in, so I told her. I didn't think there was anything wrong with that because growing up my family encouraged me to be who I was and share what I thought and believed. I wouldn't tell her or anyone that they were going to hell.

When we went back to school, it felt like none of the girls would look or even talk to me, and when they did talk to me, they did the "Sammy Sprinkler" and spit on me. They were mad at me because of what Jane had told them. They were mean because Jane had lied and misled them and her parents about what really happened. It had more to do with the lie that Jane had told, than my religion itself. They thought I told Jane that she was "going to hell," when really, I just told her what I believed when she asked. I did not expect to get treated the way I did. Getting treated like this for a lie about something that was a part of who I was took a crack at my confidence. It was hard to go to school when her dad was my teacher, and it felt like everyone was ignoring me because they believed Jane.

I went to talk to the counselor and told her what was going on. I told her how hurt, confused, and left out I felt. She told me that she was friends with the girl's dad and believed that those girls would never act that way. I felt more alone than I had before. I cried a lot, and it shook me that a lie about what was said had this big of a backlash.

My parents did not really know what to say to help me, besides telling me that it was brave of me to share what I believed. They told me that they were proud of me.

I decided to reach out to my pastor's wife. I told her how upset I was that I was being treated like this, just for sharing my beliefs. I told her I didn't understand. She helped me remember that this is what I choose to believe. Not everyone is going to believe the same or approve of what I believe. But I have to decide whether I would let what other people think, dictate what I do.

It was really hard, but I was not going to stop believing in God just because of how people were treating me. I know they aren't bad people and I never looked at them that way. I just did not like their actions towards me. I was going to do my best to use how they treated me to grow my faith stronger and become more confident in who I am. Unfortunately, it seemed that because we had different beliefs, and I was left out. I still to this day get picked on for my faith, but it is a part of me.

> Faith
> *noun*
> 1. complete trust or confidence in someone or something.

You believe what you believe, and I believe what I believe. Right? The only way that your faith or what you believe in can be shaken is if *you* let it. Nothing or no one can have a faith or a belief for you. As you figure out what you believe in, it is important to know *why* you believe what you believe. People are going to disagree with you. That is okay and should be expected. However, I believe that no matter if you and I believe the same or differently, I want you to know that you are loved and accepted just as you are.

You will never impact the world by being like it.

There will be people who don't like you and disagree with you, and it hurts and stinks. But don't let other people hold you back from sharing your truth. If your truth can help someone and bring him or her comfort, it is important for you to always confidently speak your truth, even though it might mean some people won't like you. This circumstance was one of the first times I realized that not everyone will agree with or accept me for who I am. I also realized that the truth is still the truth even if no one believes it, and a lie is still a lie even if everyone believes it.

Honestly, going through middle school was a lot harder than I thought it was going to be. There were times when people were mean or said mean things to me that crushed my spirit. No matter how much you think you like or love yourself, words will still hurt. People leaving you out and spreading rumors will still hurt. The point of this book is not to take away the hurt, because I can't. Believe me, if I could, I would bear all the hurt in the world for your precious soul. The point is to help you get through the hurt because the hurt will come. I believe that some of the things I have gone through can help you. I believe that there is a purpose in my pain. I want you to know that no matter how hard things get or how hurt you are, you get to decide how you use your pain. There is a purpose for what you are going through. I want to speak my truth and help you speak yours.

Bullying is something that happens in every school. It is becoming a huge problem. I don't really think schools or parents know how to get it under control, but honestly, I think that the problem goes deeper than that. It goes deep down to the mental health and self-worth of both the teenagers and bullies. The reason bullying exists is that hurt, and insecurities exist, and sometimes we don't know what to do with the feelings, so we take them out on others.

Bullying is never okay, but I have learned that bullies are hurting worse than they are hurting others. *Hurt people hurt people.* Maybe they have a hard family life that you don't know about. Maybe they don't like themselves. Maybe there is something about you that they like and are jealous of, so they are mean to you. Almost always, being bullied has nothing to do with you. It has everything to do with the bully. Remember how we talked about self-talk and feelings? How you treat others is a direct reflection of how you treat and talk to yourself. If someone is judgmental and critical of you, they are 100x more critical and judgmental of themselves.

False Confidence

I like to think of bullying as "false confidence." Many people think you either have confidence, or you don't. But I think you either have true confidence or false confidence. False confidence is tearing others down to feel good about yourself. When people don't find value in themselves the value they see in others scares them and makes them feel intimidated. Instead of finding value in themselves, they try to strip others of their value. They try to unscrew someone else's light bulb to try to make their own shine.

Comparison is a form of false confidence. Bullying is a form of false confidence. It is false confidence because for a little while after you tear someone down, you feel better about yourself. "At least I'm not as bad as they are," you think. But this only lasts for so long, until you feel insecure again and you tear another person down to feel better about yourself. True confidence isn't found by tearing others down. It is found in loving who you are and building that person up.

If you, or someone you know, is experiencing bullying, please talk to a trusted adult. If you see someone getting bullied, please speak up. If you have bullied or are currently bullying someone, please reach out and make things right. Being bullied will affect someone's heart more than you think it does. Do your part. Next time you feel the need to be mean to someone, take a deeper look at what inside of you is hurting. It is never okay to tear other people down, especially yourself. I know how easy it is to get sucked in. Start with being kind to yourself and slowly it will become easier to be kind to those around you.

How to Handle Bullies

A lot of people ask me how to handle bullies. You probably aren't going to like my answer, but this is what I have learned over the years.

1. Ignore them.

They are looking for a reaction out of you. If you freak out, cry, start rumors, or try to get revenge on them, you are stooping to their level and giving them what they want. They will know that they can get to you, and next time they will come at you harder.

Don't get me wrong; sometimes you need to stand up for yourself. Tell them what they said wasn't very nice, tell them they are being mean. But there are some battles not worth fighting, and sometimes walking away and leaving it be, is the best thing to do for your heart.

2. Kill them with kindness

I wrote earlier that "hurt people hurt people." The people who hurt the most are the ones who need the most love. It will make you feel better by being nice to them. It will make them look bad for being mean to you. It might help them realize how crappy they are acting.

Maybe try a few compliments on the mean people around you. Their hearts are the unhappiest, and they too need love and kindness.

"Do not say 'I will repay evil' wait for the Lord and HE will deliver you."

Proverbs 20:6

---

3. **What is said about you is NONE of your business.**

What a person says behind your back is none of your business. Read that again. What a person says behind your back is none of your business. I know it is addictive to want to know who said what, and what they think of you. But what they think and say is none of your business. You can't control it. At the end of the day, knowing hurts you more than it helps you. Who cares what they think and say? What matters is what you think and say about yourself. This will help you focus more on loving yourself than being loved by others. That is what really matters here.

So, the next time someone comes up to gossip about what so-and-so said about you, tell them, "No, thanks." Tell them that you don't want to know and that it is none of your business. If you are feeling feisty, ask that person what they said in return to stand up for you. If they were a true friend, they would stick up for you and stop the gossip.

4. Talk about it.

Let your parents, grandparents, aunt, uncle, counselor, principal, or someone that you trust know what is happening. It is okay to be hurt, upset, cry, freak out, or punch a pillow. But don't do it in public, and don't flip out at the bullies. You can try writing them a mean letter and never giving it to them, but it might help get out some of the feelings you feel.

Also, try having a conversation with your bully. We talked about communicating your feelings, and maybe they don't realize that what they are doing is hurting you. Perhaps they don't know how *much* it hurts you. I would suggest asking them if you can talk to them (in private, in person) and say, "Hey is everything okay? What you say about me/do to me really hurts my feelings. I just want you to know that. It would be really cool if you could stop what you are doing because what you're doing isn't cool." Only pull them aside and tell them your feelings one time. After that, if it keeps happening, that's when you need to get an adult involved.

5. It is NOT about you.

Your being bullied is NOT about you. It has nothing to do with you. You are good enough, pretty enough, smart enough, and you *are* enough. Nothing that anyone says or does to you will change that. Remember, how people treat you is a direct reflection of how they treat themselves. Yikes, right? You are worthy of love and good friends. Nothing is wrong with you. Fight those negative thoughts placed in your head by those who are negative about them-selves. They don't deserve room in your pretty mind. Let it hurt, cry about it, and write about it. You don't deserve this. Wipe your tears. Write some affirmations and remind yourself who you are. Don't let people who don't like themselves cause you to not like yourself.

There is always going to be someone who does not see your worth. Don't let it be you.

It is important to catch yourself and to pay attention to what you are thinking. Your thoughts run your life. What you think becomes what you do. Your self-talk, comparison, identity, and feelings all stem from whether you have true confidence or false confidence.

I know it is hard. It sucks. I know you want it all to end and go away. I know you want to walk through the halls without worrying about what will be said to you. I know you want to come home without feeling like crying. I am so sorry that this is happening. I have been there. You are not alone. If anything, please use me as proof that you can get through this. I have fought the fight that you are fighting. I am still overcoming it. I am right here with you, holding your hand, rooting for you, and praying for your heart.

Ideas to remember from this chapter:

1. In what ways do you act out of false confidence?

_____

_____

_____

_____

_____

_____

_____

2. Have you been bullied, or been a bully? How has it affected you?

_____

_____

_____

_____

_____

_____

_____

3. Is there someone you need to tell how you are feeling? Practice writing what you would say.

_____

_____

_____

_____

_____

_____

_____

_____

4. Write three things you are proud of.

_____

_____

_____

_____

_____

_____

_____

_____

Bela's Answers

1. I act out in false confidence when I compare and when I believe the lies in my head. I have to try to be cautious of what I let myself think or I will spiral, fast.

2. Growing up I was super negative, struggled with bad attitudes and being bratty. I was not always positive or the nicest. I also had people who were not nice to me and it really affected how I thought about and treated myself. Now, all of this has caused me to do my best to be kind to all and to try to help others. Each day I do my best to speak kindly to myself, even when it's hard.

3. To my friend who really hurt my feelings:
   Sometimes the words you say to me are really hurtful. When I try to talk to you about it, you don't listen, or you blame me. You are important to me and I love you but I don't want to be your friend if you can't be nicer to me. I forgive you, but we might have to spend some time apart for me to heal.

I am proud of myself:

4.
- for taking bad situations and using them for good.
- for being kinder to myself than I used to be.
- for the strength I have within me.

CHAPTER EIGHT

Personal Boundaries

> Personal Boundaries
> *noun*
> 1. limits that show reasonable ways for other people
> to behave towards you or treat you and how you will
> respond when someone passes those limits.

S etting boundaries is loving yourself by saying "no" to things that hurt you, and "yes" to things that serve you. You need boundaries because they protect your heart from things that aren't the best for you and hurt you. To be able to set boundaries, you first need to start paying attention to the way things make you feel. For example, the way you feel after hanging out with certain friends or family members, after you eat certain foods, after watching or listening to media, and what you do after all of these encounters. Boundaries can be placed on anything that harms you. If you don't take time to recognize what harms you, then you won't know what to protect yourself from. It'll be like swinging at a piñata blindfolded, hoping you hit what is there.

In order to protect your heart, you need to know what is hurting it. To be honest, as I promised I would be, I didn't know about the concept of boundaries until a few years ago. I thought that I *had* to go places, hang out with people, and do things even if they felt off or I didn't want to. I would get a feeling in my stomach that something wasn't right, or that I did not want to go and do things, but I ignored it and did anyway. Maybe that's you. Let me tell you something, if something feels wrong or off, there is a good chance it *is*. Setting boundaries means it is okay to say "no."

Setting Boundaries with Friends

Imagine having a girl regularly ask you to hang out, and because you don't want to be rude, you say yes, and hang out. While hanging out all she does is talk about herself, or say rude comments to you, and gossip about other people. After hanging out with her, you always feel tired, drained, and negative. But you feel that have to hang out with her. Right?

Listen, pretty girl, if hanging out with someone costs you your peace, positivity, or energy, is that really the kind of person you want to be hanging out with? If you feel gross after hanging out with someone, that is your gut telling you that they aren't helping you, they are hurting you. Only you can feel your gut feelings. Only you know how others make you feel and what makes you uncomfortable. Try to practice saying "no" to things that don't fill your cup, and spend more time doing things that do.

You do not need to be a doormat. Be a door holder. It is okay to welcome things and people, but sometimes the door needs to close.

Sometimes when setting boundaries, we have to set them between ourselves and another person. Maybe that means we don't talk to them as much, we don't follow them on social media, or maybe we aren't even friends anymore. You need to make the best decision that truly helps your heart, even if it is hard. Setting boundaries does not include gossiping about other people. It is politely pulling back with the best intentions for you and that person.

I had a friend in middle school who I shared everything with. Her name was Karen. She was always the first person I told my news too, good and bad. There was nothing we didn't talk about. Shortly after I would tell her things, I noticed that everyone else would know about them too. I knew she was the only person I had been telling. I was very upset and crushed because I thought Karen was one of my best friends. But best friends don't reveal secrets. I really did not want everyone to know what I had been telling her. I was tired of my secrets being shared around the school, so I had to decide if I was going to keep telling her stuff after she proved multiple times that she could not keep a secret, OR if I was going to love myself enough to create a boundary.

I started not to tell Karen stuff anymore because it hurt me more than it helped me. I would still talk to her and hang out with her, but I just simply chose not to tell her things that I did not want everyone to know. This was when I started being picky about what I shared. I learned that at the end of the day it is my heart on the line, not the person that I am telling. I needed to be wise with what I shared. I found sharing things with my mom really helped me.

When setting this boundary, I did not walk up to Karen and tell her that I was going to stop telling her things. I simply took time to pay attention to how I felt and what would be the best for my heart, and then I created a boundary within myself. An agreement with myself that I was done telling Karen my secrets. She had no idea about my decision. It was an agreement with myself to honor how I felt when my secrets were being told and a decision not to feel that way any longer. So, I set internal boundaries for myself on how much I would share, and I stuck to them.

This way my heart hurt a lot less and my secrets were not all over school. Distancing and setting boundaries can be hard because you may have to let go of something you are used to having or that is comfortable. It may feel weird or uncomfortable for a while, but it is always worth it to give up things that weigh heavy on your heart. For me, it was really hard to distance myself from a friend I use to tell everything to, someone who walked around knowing all of my secrets. I knew I owed it to myself to find a friend who would love and respect me enough to keep my secrets, and I wasn't going to settle for a friend that would not.

Setting Boundaries with Family Members

Other examples of boundaries are those that I have learned to set with parts of my family. It was very hard for me to learn that sometimes family members can be toxic and hurt my heart too. I always thought family was supposed to be a safe, positive place. For me, and many other people families, however, may not be the most positive place. I just want you to know that if you have a toxic family member or someone within your family is hurtful to you; it is okay to set reasonable boundaries with them.

When I would go to my grandma's to hang out with my birth dad's side of the family, I would come home feeling depressed and exhausted. There was something about being around them that drained me, and I did not enjoy it. I would always cry when I came home because everything was fine when I was there, and they seemed like they wanted to be part of my life. After I left, they would not talk to me or make an effort to be in my life. Being there was like living in a false reality and coming home was like waking up from a perfect dream and feeling empty because it would never come true.

Obviously, I loved them, and it made me sad to feel like this. I hoped that I would be able to go over there and be fine afterward, but still each time I felt gross when I came home. It hurt me to feel this way each time. I had to decide whether I wanted to allow myself to keep feeling like that or if I loved myself enough to set a boundary for my best interest. I was not rude about it, but I slowly stopped going over there as much. This was really hard because part of me did not want them to be mad at me for not spending time with them.

I would go on occasion because I felt like I had to, but it was perfectly okay for me to decline their offer in a polite way because I was protecting my heart. Once again, I did not call them and tell them that I was deciding to set boundaries. I took how I felt when I was around them into consideration, talked to my parents about it, and set a boundary for myself. I had to think long and hard if I wanted to spend my time feeling crappy and hurt, or if I was going to do something about it, so I could be happier and not hurt as much. Boundaries are strictly to protect your heart, mind, and body, and to love yourself enough stay out of harmful situations that can be avoided.

Setting Boundaries with Myself

I learned that not all boundaries are about our heart and mind. For me, I use to get sick a lot. I would feel like I was getting stabbed in the guts. I would get pounding headaches, feel brain fog, and always feel tired after eating. I felt like crap all the time, and I thought it was normal. Finally, I went to a nutritionist, and she said she thought that I need to be gluten-free. I was not happy about this because I love everything that contains gluten, from bread to cakes, to Doritos. Gluten was my jam. But I was absolutely sick and tired of literally being sick and tired, so I decided to give this gluten-free thing a try.

That was seven years ago. I am now gluten and dairy-free because my stomach cannot handle either of them and that is why I would get so sick. People use to make fun of me and make comments about my not eating gluten and dairy, saying that it was only so I could lose weight and be skinnier. I was made fun of for what I could and couldn't eat. How ridiculous is that? It hurt my feelings at first because there was *nothing* I could do about it. I knew I could not eat those foods without feeling sick. Then I realized the best thing I could do was to listen to my body and feed it the foods that make it feel good.

Every once in a while, just like I thought I could see my birth dad's side without feeling gross after, I would think that maybe I could eat gluten and not get sick. Each time I would be wrong and would regret it every time. Each time that I thought that maybe the things that were previously toxic weren't anymore, and maybe I could handle them, I would get hurt worse than before. I realized that I would rather be without that food than feel the way I felt. Each day, I made the choice to love myself enough to not hurt my body and instead to love it and give it what it needed. If something makes you physically, mentally, or emotionally sick, love yourself enough to listen to what your mind, body, and heart are telling you.

Sometimes you won't get physically sick, but you will experience a sick feeling in your stomach. You know that feeling when you know you said something or did something you shouldn't have, and your heart drops, and you feel sick? Yeah, that. That is your gut telling you "Oh crap, don't do that again." These feelings are there to show us what we need to learn from. Your inner voice and gut feelings are pretty much always right when it comes to things that are hurting you.

You can either live life one tap at a time, or you can wait to get punched. By this I mean, your gut/discernment will always give you a little feeling when things aren't right. It is like a tap saying, "Hey, I don't like that." It is subtle but hard to miss because it makes you aware that something is off. Now, it will only tap you for so long. The more you fight it off, the stronger it becomes. If you don't listen, it will evolve from a tap into a hard nudge, "HEY, I don't like that." Then from there, when your gut is screaming at you that something isn't right, it will eventually punch you in the face, so you cannot hide or push down the feelings anymore. "HEY, I TOLD YOU I DON'T LIKE THAT," it will say. You get to choose whether you listen to the taps and honor yourself OR wait to get punched in the face. Either way, that feeling in your gut will not go away. It has your best interests at heart and is trying to protect you. You can set boundaries for yourself on how much you are going to allow yourself to go past the feeling that something is wrong. How much you are going to put up with things that hurt you. You have the choice to protect yourself.

Sometimes you need to say "no" to protect yourself from harmful situations. It is perfectly okay for you to say no to something without feeling bad. You can say no to things that aren't necessarily bad, as well. Something is bad if it hurts you, even if it is a "good" thing. If you have that gut feeling that a person, situation, or place is not right, then say "no" out of love for yourself. The only person who knows how you truly feel is you. This is why communication is so important; talking to an adult you trust, letting them know how you feel, and then coming up with a solution that is best for you.

I had a very hard time learning to say "no" without feeling bad because I didn't want to hurt other peoples feelings. I cared so much about pleasing them that I allowed myself to remain in toxic, harmful situations that could have been avoided if I would have said "no." It is important to make sure that *when you are saying "yes" to something that you are not saying "no" to yourself.*

False Guilt

One thing that made it very hard for me to set boundaries and be okay with saying "no," is something I didnt even know existed : my nemesis, false guilt. This is something that I have struggled with my whole life and that I still struggle with to this day. It is being able to separate true and false guilt. So, what is true guilt? True guilt is a good thing. You feel guilty when you lie, when you punch your siblings, or when you do something that you know you should not have done. When you experience true guilt, it is a good thing and can help you correct any wrong you have done or harm you have caused and learn from it. False guilt is when you feel guilty but have done nothing wrong.

For example, false guilt can appear when you say "no" to hanging out with a friend, say "no" to going to a party, or not eating something because you don't want to feel sick. You can feel false guilt because of how you look, or because of how people react to you, treat you or view you. You might feel false guilt for resting after you have worked your butt off. These are all situations that should not lead to guilt. False guilt can cause you to say that you are sorry for something that you didn't even do, or something that hurt you. It can lead you to compromise yourself in order not to hurt others' feelings. It can also lead you to be a part of toxic relationships and in harmful situations, because you feel bad about saying "no."

False guilt can prevent you from setting healthy boundaries and keep you in unhealthy, unhappy situations. It will keep you stuck. Next time you are feeling guilty, ask yourself, "Did I really do anything wrong?" and "Is there something I need to make right or apologize for?" Keep in mind that you never have to apologize for protecting your heart and doing what is best for you. You never have to apologize for being who you are. Usually, false guilt attacks you when you are trying to be strong, make a change, or love yourself more. False guilt wants you to stay sad, hurt, and broken. It does not want you to change and be better. If you become better and stronger, it will have less power over you. Guilt, on the other hand, wants you to make things right and to acknowledge the wrong you have done. The reason the word "no" was invented was to use when something doesnt feel good or right to you. This is another reason why being aware of your feelings is so important. Remember it is good to be aware of them, but not to live in them.

I always felt like I had to explain myself when I set boundaries. Some people would get offended that I wouldn't allow them to treat me poorly anymore. Some people got offended that I no longer went to places that didn't feel right or that I didn't want to hang out with them anymore. Others didn't like it when I changed because it forces them to question if they should be changing too. The only person you need to explain your boundaries to is yourself, God, and a trusted adult or therapist.

At the end of the day, remember that no one in this world knows what your gut is telling you, except you. No one can tell you what your gut should feel. No one can change what it feels. You feel what you feel, and that is okay. But make sure you are paying attention to when you experience those feelings that something isn't right, because most of the time, it isn't. You have to be able to lay your head down at night and live with the things you allow in your life. At the end of the day, I hope you love yourself enough to walk away from things that are hurting you and run towards the things that will heal you.

It is hard to let go of our normal. Some of the things that are the worst for us, we are super attached too almost as if they were a habit. It is painful to say "no" to a part of yourself. Each of us has the ability to be incredibly powerful and positive, or dark and negative. Whichever side you give the most attention to, and feed, will become who you are.

- You have a choice in what you put up with.
- You are so incredibly strong.
- You have so much power in you.
- You are loved beyond measure.
- I am here with you, each day fighting this battle to become our best selves.
- You are not alone.
- Each step and choice you make gets you a little closer to who you were made to be.

Set those boundaries, protect your heart, and be kind to yourself and others.

Ideas to remember from this chapter:

1. What are some things that are hurting your heart?

_____

_____

_____

_____

_____

_____

_____

2. What do you need to say "no" to?

_____

_____

_____

_____

_____

_____

_____

_____

3. Do you have boundaries in your life?

_____

_____

_____

_____

_____

_____

_____

4. Where do you need to set boundaries in your life?

_____

_____

_____

_____

_____

_____

_____

_____

5. Do you experience false guilt? What does it make you feel guilty about?

_____

_____

_____

_____

_____

_____

_____

_____

6. What are three things that make your heart happy?

    1. _____

    2. _____

    3. _____

7. Spend more time doing those things.

Bela's Answers

1. Right now social media is hurting my heart. Seeing other people's lives and comparing mine is exhausting. I sometimes feel like I need to perform or prove myself in order to be accepted or "good enough."

2. I need to be better at who I spend time on and who I allow in my life. I also am going to take time off of social media to quiet my mind and take time for myself.

3. I have boundaries on what things I will share with certain people. I am picky with who I tell things to. I also like and need alone time to recharge so I have boundaries to allow myself to have "me time."

4. I need to set boundaries on the amount of time I spend on social media. I also need to get better at the boundaries I have set with certain people.

5. I personally experience false guilt a ton. Usually it makes me feel bad about saying no. Whether it's saying no to going somewhere or hanging out with someone, I feel bad about it and often have to remind myself that it is okay to say no.

6.
- The sun
- Music
- Dressing nicely

CHAPTER NINE
Acceptance

> Acceptance
> *noun*
> 1. a person's ability to recognize reality without attempting to change it or protest it.

I struggle a lot with acceptance in my life. I always like to wish things were different or create an image of how they should be in my head. Sometimes I can trick myself into thinking something is different than it is, into thinking things are the way I want them to be, but that never changes the reality of them.

I did not know what acceptance truly was until I was fourteen. So, I have been working on relearning how to accept things. Before I was fourteen, I thought that acceptance meant that I was okay with the circumstances in my life. That I had to be okay with being bullied. That I had to be okay with the fact that my birth dad was not in my life. I just thought that I could never be bothered or hurt, and I had to be okay with it all.

This led to my getting very angry at myself because no matter how I tried, I could never make myself be okay with my deep hurts, or with the people who caused them. I thought something must be wrong with me. Why the heck was it so hard to accept the way things REALLY were in my life? Why did I always have to alter them?

I've been in therapy since I was five. It turns out that the first therapist I had would always tell me to accept things and deal with them, but never really gave me the tools to do so. She would regularly tell me to accept things and that then I would be able to move past them. Bless her soul, I know she meant well but I spent ten years of my life going to therapy, and I still did not know what acceptance was or how the heck to accept things.

When I moved schools going into ninth grade, I changed to a different therapist who was closer to my new school. Sitting in a chair, squeezing a stress ball, I told her a brief overview of what had happened in my life so far and why I was in therapy in the first place. I told her that I just needed to accept everything and then I would be okay, everything would be great. I said this all in a mocking voice because the thought of accepting anything was way beyond me because I still hadn't managed to be able to.

She looked at me with kind eyes, and said "Bela, do you even know what acceptance is?" I told her that it was being okay with everything in my life, not bothered by it anymore. She then went on to explain that acceptance has nothing to do with being okay with everything, or not being bothered. You don't have to like something, approve, or be okay with something in order to accept it. She told me that I could be bothered and angry about things and still have accepted them. This whole time I felt like something was wrong with me because I couldn't accept anything. That whole time, I couldn't accept anything because I was holding myself to impossible expectations, something no one would ever be able to do. I was wrong, and I was so happy that I was wrong because that day I felt free. I will never forget the day she told me what real acceptance is.

Acceptance is recognizing your reality. In the chapter about rejection, I talked about my birth dad and how he left when I was five. For the longest time, I had a false reality in my head about the great dad that he was. I had memories of us giggling, snuggling, and having fun. I focused so much on those memories that I refused to focus on how things really were – my actual reality.

My reality was (and still is to this day) that I have a dad who did not want to be my dad. He has never made an effort to be in my life. He does not know my favorite colors, movies, pictures, outfits, or jokes. He has never met any of my friends or watched me play a single sports game. He has not witnessed me break down after coming home from a tough day at school. He has not witnessed my heartbreak from a boy. He is not here. He is not a good dad to me. I know he loves me, but he is not part of my life.

For years I tried to do everything I could to change this reality. I would hold in my feelings about him. I would never say "no," so he wouldn't get mad. I would try to make him love me and want to be my dad. I would picture how things were supposed to be, and I would refuse to look at the way things really were. I felt, and still sometimes feel, like I am not good enough, and I struggle with negative self-talk. I feel like I need to earn people's love, and I struggle with comparing myself to the love that others get. I struggle with being okay when people no longer want to be a part of my life because for so long I linked people leaving with me with my not being good enough. I struggle with putting up boundaries to protect myself because I don't like to hurt other people's feelings, even when they are hurting mine.

I had unrealistic expectations. I thought maybe one day he would come home and decide to be a dad, and everything would click and work out. I expected him to want to get to know me and to make time for me. I expected him to move home. I was disappointed when none of this came true, and I thought it was all my fault. I felt rejected because I was trying to take responsibility for his actions when they had absolutely nothing to do with me. There is nothing I could do to change his choices because they were his choices, not mine.

Acceptance is letting go of everything you can't control and focusing on what you can. Trying to control things that you can't is draining and will leave you unhappy every time because there is *nothing* you can do. No matter how much you worry, cry, or obsess over the things you cannot control, nothing will change them. It is what it is. It's not good or bad, it just is. So instead, taking control of the things that you can control is powerful, and it shows you that you do have a choice in your life and what you do with it.

Here are some things you can control:

Your decisions	What you say
How you spend your time	Who you hang out with
Your thoughts	What you believe
How you treat others	Your attitude
How you react	How you deal with things

Things you cannot control:

Who your family is	What others say
What you look like	Who others hang out with
What others think about you	What others believe
How others treat you	Others' feelings & attitudes
Your circumstances	Your past

I struggled with accepting how I looked for the longest time. I never *hated* how I looked, besides the time that I told you about when there was the rumor that I had gotten a boob job. Other than that time, I always thought I was pretty, and I didn't mind the way that I looked. After the whole "boob job" rumor, I questioned myself and struggled to accept the way my body was. I thought maybe if I wore baggy shirts they wouldn't be there, or I could hide them. That didn't change the fact that they were still there and that I couldn't control them. I tried so hard to control what I looked like or to alter it, but at the end of the day tearing myself down and trying to hide part of myself, just made me feel really insecure and made me not like myself. If I felt like I needed to hide part of me so others would like me, did I really accept myself? I know that you don't need to like something to accept it, but I really wanted to like who I was and everything about myself. If I am being honest, I believe everyone has something that they don't like about them-selves.

That's when I started amplifying my flaws. Instead of wearing baggy shirts I wore fitted ones. I started accepting who I was and what I looked like. I was done hiding from it. Yes, my insecurity was totally still there, and honestly still is to this day. Instead of running from it, I faced it and said, "Alright this is the way things are, I cannot do anything about it." I wasn't wearing tight shirts to show off, I was doing it for myself. Something in my head clicked, and I liked myself more because I wasn't running from my reality.

Do you remember the story I told you about my former best friend who I told all of my secrets? I had a really hard time accepting that she was not the friend that I thought she was. I thought maybe I was a bad friend, or maybe she didn't like me as much as I thought she did. I wanted to control the friendship. I wanted her to be a better friend, so we could remain friends, but she wasn't able to. So, I had to accept the reality of the type of friend she was. I had to accept that she did not live up to the type of friend I imagined her to be in my mind.

Sometimes acceptance comes with setting boundaries. I set a boundary with her that I would no longer tell her secrets. I set a boundary with my birth dad to not have contact with him because he was not the dad that I needed. When I decided I was going to do my best each day to accept myself, I set boundaries for how I was going to allow myself to speak to myself. This helps us control what we can control.

I have struggled with acceptance in other areas of my life as well. It is hard to teach yourself to accept things but the more you practice it, the easier it gets. Acceptance is not just something that you do once, and then you're done. The truth is, the thing you are accepting is going to pop back in your brain, and you're going to have to decide if you are going to accept it again or if you're going to try to control and change it again. It is a daily battle, and sometimes even a minute-by-minute challenge. It takes saying "no" to your self-talk and not allowing yourself to "think" yourself into a bad mood.

Every day at school, practice accepting how people treat you, what they say, who they are, who their friends are, their attitude, and accepting who you are. Instead of trying to change things, just take a second to yourself to think through the reality of the situation. Once you stop trying to control how everything is and realize that only a few things are in your control, you will feel so much freedom. You won't care as much about what people say or think about you because you cannot control it. My mom always says:

———————— •❦• ————————

"You can be the ripest peach in the world, but there is always going to be someone who doesn't like peaches."

———————— •❦• ————————

Meaning that no matter how hard you try to please everyone or get everyone to like you, it will never happen. The people who are meant to be in your life will always be there. If someone isn't part of your life anymore it is because they have served their purpose and they are no longer needed. This does not make it any easier. This does not make it hurt any less. Please hear me when I say, the way someone treats you has nothing to do with you. If someone is no longer in your life or isn't making an effort — that is their choice, not yours. There is nothing you can do about it. People's attitudes towards you are not your responsibility. People's words about you or to you have nothing to do with you, and everything to do with them.

I don't know what your life looks like. I don't know what you are going through or have gone through. I don't know how you deal with things. I do know that it is okay to not be okay. It is okay to be hurt, to have bad days, to cry, to be angry, and it is okay to want things to be different. This is your only life. You cannot waste it wishing you were someone else, or that you had something that you don't or that what happened to you didn't happen, because it did. That is reality. Who you are, who your family is, and your past is your reality. I know there are things you want to change. I know there are things that make you sick to your stomach when you think about them. I know you wish you did not have to hurt like this and go through this pain.

I do too. I wish there was something we could do to change it all, to make things the way we wished they would be, to control other people and make them want us or be our friends, or to change our flaws instead of having to wake up and fight ourselves to love them each day. But we can't. We aren't alone in this. I don't think anyone in this world can say that their life went exactly how they wanted it too or how they planned it. Things happen, things change. It is what it is. We need to let go of the illusion of how things *should* be. Because they are not that way. Things are the way they are, and that is how they are supposed to be.

You and I are right where we need to be. What we are going through is making us who we are created to be. This hurt, pain, and confusion will all make sense someday because nothing is ever wasted, not even a single tear. You do not have to be okay with what has happened to you, or what you have gone through. You can be bothered. But you can't sit and obsess over it and wish it was different. When we run from reality, we become insecure and deeply hurt.

- There is a purpose for your pain.
- There is a purpose for your life.
- You are needed in this world.
- Exactly who you are is perfect and loved.
- You are exactly who you are created to be.
- You are a masterpiece.
- There is only one you and there will never be another one just like you.
- You don't have to be pretty like her, be pretty like you.

Ideas to remember from this chapter:

1. Did you know what acceptance was before reading this?

_____

_____

_____

_____

_____

_____

_____

_____

2. What are some things you struggle with accepting?

_____

_____

_____

_____

_____

_____

_____

_____

_____

3. How are you going to start to accept things today?

_____

_____

_____

_____

_____

_____

_____

4. Write three things you like about the way you look.

1. _____

2. _____

3. _____

Bela's Answers

1. I always love reading this chapter to refresh my mind on what acceptance is.

2. I still struggle with accepting the reality of my Birth dad. Some days it hits me harder than others and it is something I will struggle to accept each day, But I'll do my best.

3. To help me better accept things I'm going to remind myself of the things I can and cannot control. I tend to try to control everything and it gets exhausting.

4.
   - my eyes
   - my smile
   - my dimples

CHAPTER TEN

Forgiveness

> Forgiveness
> *noun*
> 1. a conscious, intentional decision to release feelings of resentment or vengeance toward a person or group who has hurt you, whether or not they actually deserve your forgiveness.

Every single person in your life will hurt you somehow. Maybe not on purpose, but something they say or do will hurt your feelings. When you are hurt, you have the option to hold on to that hurt, think about it constantly, hold it over their heads, and remind them all of the time, or you have the choice to forgive them.

I struggled with acceptance the same way I struggled with forgiveness. I had an idea of what forgiveness was, but I wasn't sure. When talking about forgiveness, I think it is super important to talk about what forgiveness is NOT. I know I struggled with false ideas of forgiveness, and so has every other person that I have met.

Let's start with what is not forgiveness.
Forgiveness is NOT:

- Lessening what happened
- Saying what happened is okay or excusing it
- Forgetting
- Not being hurt anymore
- Being weak
- Repairing a relationship

We tend to think that when we forgive it means that we don't take what they did seriously. We think that we are saying it is okay or that we are going to forget about it. I personally struggled with the idea that I could forgive someone and still be hurt by what they did. I thought I had to be okay and unbothered, but forgiveness does not change what happened. Our society likes to say that if we forgive, we are weak, but actually forgiving takes a lot of strength and is one of the most powerful things a person can do. Forgiveness does not mean that you have to let that person back into your life.

For me, unforgiveness is not an option. I have seen the effects of unforgiveness in my life. I have felt my heart harden. I have become bitter and paralyzed with hurt. Forgiveness is so important because *unforgiveness is like drinking poison and hoping that someone else dies*. Unforgiveness hurts you more than it hurts the person you are not forgiving. It will damage *your* heart and *your* ability to love, not theirs. Your forgiving them or not forgiving them does not affect their heart at all, only yours.

In order to be able to love ourselves and others correctly, we need to be able to forgive. This means we need to forgive *everyone* that hurts us. Even if they are not sorry. This is one of the hardest things to do. Forgiveness is not for them. It is for you to move on and be able to hold more love than hurt.

Forgiveness is not just saying "I forgive you." It is choosing in your heart to forgive them. The only way it will be true forgiveness is if you forgive in your heart. Forgiveness is *choosing* **not** to hurt someone just because they have hurt you. Forgiveness is *choosing* **not** to hold something over someone's head and bring it up regularly to remind them of when they hurt you or when they screwed up. Forgiveness is *choosing* to let go of the hurt and *choosing* not to allow those feelings to run your life.

Many people think that once you forgive, you are automatically over it and you have let go. That is not true. Forgiveness is a daily choice. Trust me, the hurt will come back up, and you will remember what they did and how bad they hurt you. You will be tempted to bring it back up and remind them. Forgiveness is choosing not to bring it back up. When you forgive someone, you not only stop holding your hurt over the person's head, you stop gossiping to others about what was done to you and how much hurt it caused you. Forgiveness is being kind and showing love to those who have hurt you. Forgiveness is *not something that is earned*. It is something that is *given* out of love and grace. It is being strong enough to set the hurt down and pick up love, over and over.

Forgiving Yourself
The hardest person to forgive is yourself. Like I said, in order to love correctly you have to let go of the hurt. This includes the hurt you have given yourself too. I know you have done things that have hurt yourself. You have allowed people in your life who were hurtful to you, and you have disappointed yourself. You have lied to yourself. You have let yourself be treated less than you deserve. You have been mean to yourself, doubted yourself, and torn yourself down. Maybe you didn't live up to expectations, whatever the excuse, there is nothing in this world that you could ever do that would make you unlovable, or not good enough.

Here are some ways that you hurt yourself when you can't forgive yourself:
- You keep reminding yourself what you did
- You let it affect your decisions
- You feel paralyzed
- You tear yourself down with negative self-talk
- You make yourself feel unworthy
- You don't try to make things better because you don't think you deserve to have things better
- You struggle to forgive others
- You struggle to trust yourself

Since we are all human, we will all mess up and hurt someone. We will even do things that hurt our own feelings. Everyone in this world needs forgiveness because not a single person on this earth is perfect. So, if you want the space to be able to live and be yourself while making mistakes and bouncing back from them, you need to make space for others to live and be human and bounce back. If you want to be forgiven when you mess up and hurt others' feelings, then you need to forgive others when they mess up and hurt your feelings.

Forgiveness will give you the freedom to live freely in love, instead of walking around in chains of hurt. Sometimes holding on hurts worse than letting go. On the next page is a drawing that I drew that represents what happens when we don't forgive. When you hold on to something so tightly, it can start to consume you.

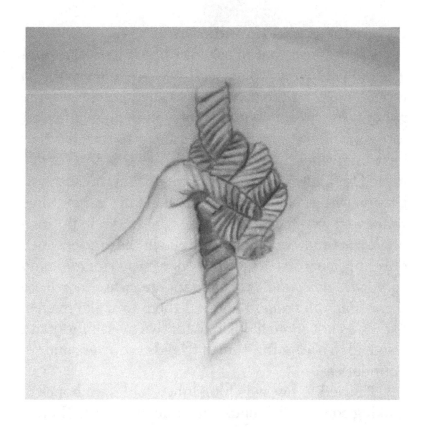

There is nothing too big or too small for forgiveness. You can forgive your siblings for making a comment that hurt your feelings, or you can forgive someone for bumping into you in the hallway. You can forgive someone for spreading a rumor about you. You can forgive parents or family members for not being there for you. It is not easy to do, but neither is walking around with a bag of hurt on your back, weighing down your every step. You get to choose whether you struggle with hurt, or you struggle with love and trying to heal.

Forgiveness and Boundaries

I mentioned that in school I had a hard time and was bullied by my "friends." It was a regular battle to forgive them for the names they called me, for leaving me out, for spitting on me, for making puking noises, for ignoring me, and for everything else they did that hurt my feelings. I also realized that I had to forgive myself for allowing others to treat me that way. I stayed friends with them even though they hurt me multiple timed and were never sorry. I forgave them in my own heart over and over and tried to be in the group, which only hurt me worse. I had to forgive myself for *allowing someone who did not understand my worth to determine my value.* I allowed them to make me feel like I was not enough. I had to forgive myself for that. I also had to accept the kind of friends they were and set boundaries.

This led to my switching lunch tables, in hopes of making some real friends who valued me. I no longer tried to talk to those girls or hang out with them. This was not because I didn't like them, I simply did not like their actions towards me and others. I realized my worth, and I was no longer going to allow people to treat me less than. I was going to do my best to surround myself with people who treated me kindly, and with respect.

It was really hard to get the courage to walk away from the only friend group that I knew. It hurt worse to hold on than it did to let go and let myself grow. I still value the good times we had together because it was not always bad. In the end, the bad did outweigh the good, and it was a breath of fresh air to surround myself with real friends. I am really proud of myself for how I handled this situation.

I want you to know that you do not have to allow people in your life that hurt you. You can love someone and hate their actions. You can love someone and distance yourself from them. I did not know about boundaries, and if I had, I would have saved myself so much hurt. I would still have been civil and kind to the girls, but I wouldn't let them close to me or tell them my secrets.

Change is scary, but sometimes the price of staying the same is scarier than the actual change.

Forgiveness is a Process

Forgiveness letters helped make forgiveness easier for me. I sat down and wrote letters to people who I needed to forgive. I wrote letters to each of the girls. I included all the things that they did that hurt me, how angry I was, and how I felt. I got all of my feelings out. I could say whatever I wanted because I was never going to give them the letters; they were strictly written to help me process and get my feelings out. I have written numerous letters to my birth dad, getting all of my feelings out. You can write them to whoever you need to. They are just a way to deal with the hurt.

After you write your own forgiveness letters, you can tear them up or burn them (with an adult). Do what you need to do after writing the letters, maybe even celebrate, because you are creating so much more space in your heart for love and joy. Be proud of yourself that you are choosing to love yourself enough to let go of the things that hurt you. That is so special, and I am so proud of you.

I used to be so mean to myself and frustrated because I thought I had to heal and be okay **right now.** I thought something was wrong with me if I took time to heal or process. Taking time is perfectly okay. Being frustrated is okay. Being mean to yourself is not.

Forgiveness is a process that takes time. It will not happen overnight. Just like healing your hurt will not happen overnight either. Please remember this while you are working through things. Give yourself time and be patient. You are doing the best you can. Do not get frustrated when it takes longer to forgive someone than you thought, or longer to heal a wound than you thought. Be nice to yourself and love yourself through this process. The more love and grace you give yourself, the easier it will be and the more you will grow.

Each day we wake up, and we love others the best we can. We will forgive them when they fall short or hurt us. We will forgive ourselves when we mess up, hurt ourselves or others. We will love ourselves and encourage ourselves to do our very best. At the end of the day, your best is all you can do. We will give others room to do their best and love them exactly where they are. We will accept them for who they are instead of trying to change them. We will accept ourselves for who we are and where we are. One day at a time, we will become more and more who we are created to be. I hope you are excited to meet that girl because she is already inside of you waiting to come out.

We've got this. Let's go forgive those who hurt us, so we can love ourselves and others more. You are not alone.

I am cheering for you, and I am right there with you.

— •❚• —

You are loved.

You are enough.

You are kind.

— •❚• —

Ideas to remember from this chapter:

1. Before reading this chapter, what did you think forgiveness was?

_____

_____

_____

_____

_____

_____

_____

2. Who do you need to forgive?

_____

_____

_____

_____

_____

_____

_____

_____

3. What do you need to forgive yourself for?

_____

_____

_____

_____

_____

_____

_____

4. Write three qualities you love about yourself.

1. _____

2. _____

3. _____

5. Spend some time writing forgiveness letters. Write at least 2.

_____

_____

_____

_____

_____

_____

_____

Bela's Answers

1. I thought forgiveness meant that I wasn't mad or hurt anymore.

2. Right now I am in the process of forgiving my best friend since birth. He said some really hurtful things to me infront of people and it crushed me. I love him but I am giving myself space to heal.

3. I need to forgive myself for allowing myself to be treated poorly. I need to forgive myself for not trusting my gut and lying to myself.

4. • My ability to accept people for who they are.
   • I'm a good listener.
   • That I like to be goofy.

5. I am going to share with you a forgiveness letter I wrote to myself as an example of how you can write them too.

5. Dear Bela,

I am upset with how you have allowed yourself to be treated. I am broken-hearted that you don't see how wonderful and enough you are. I hate that you get sucked into the lies inside your head. I hate your questioning of worth. I hate that you let how others treat you, mess with how you view and treat yourself. I wish you would trust yourself. I'm tired of being angry. I'm tired of holding on to hurt and mistakes. Today, I am choosing to let go of all of this. All of the "what ifs" and "woulda, coulda, shoulda's." All of the hurt I have caused myself. All the pressure I put on myself. There is a God who died for exactly who you are, with all your brokenness and mess ups. He died so everyone could be forgiven, including you. Bela, today I forgive you for holding on to things you know harm you. For holding on to hurt and anger. I forgive you for tearing me down and for feeling not good enough. I forgive you for not trusting me.

You are more than enough. You are loved. You are more than any mistake or choice you've made. I pray that you will learn to see yourself the way the creator of the universe does. He loves you for exactly who you are in this very moment. I love you and want what's best for you.

love,
yourself. ♡

CHAPTER ELEVEN

Gratitude

> Gratitude
> *noun*
> 1. the quality of being thankful; readiness to show appreciation for and to return kindness.

Gratitude is being thankful, appreciative, and kind. I think gratitude is all about perspective. You have probably heard about the glass being half full, or half empty. Gratitude is thinking and living as if the glass is half full. The more you look for the good, the more you will find it. The more you look for the bad, the more you will find it.

Something I still struggle with to this day is having a positive attitude or gratitude. It has always been super easy for me to be down and negative. I have had to fight myself every day to be positive instead of negative. Gratitude has helped me a lot with my battle. Gratitude is the best recipe to change your emotional state or mindset.

When I feel myself starting to feel sad, dull, off, or negative, I start to think of things that I am thankful for. I might even write a list of three things that I am thankful for each morning when I wake up. The more time I spend being grateful, the more I realize just how much we have to be grateful for.

I don't want to sit and preach at you to "just be positive" because I have been fed that line a million times in my life. Every time I heard someone say that to me, I would feel a knot in my stomach and feel like screaming at them. I felt like it was their way of telling me that "it's not that bad." Or I "shouldn't be having that hard of a time" with what I was going through. I thought having gratitude meant that everything was great. That I was in a great mood, that my life was going great, that nothing was bothering me. I thought everything had to be great in order to have gratitude or be grateful. That's the beauty of it. You can have gratitude right smack dab in the middle of the mess.

Gratitude does not mean everything is okay or going great. It does not belittle what you are going through or make it any less hard. It is just a way of viewing your circumstances. You can still feel the pain and be upset. But instead of sitting and thinking yourself in circles about how bad things are or how bad you are hurting, gratitude stops the circles and gives you time to breathe. It helps you see the good in the bad.

An example that I can think of to share with you is when I lost the person I thought was my best friend.

We did everything together. Watched movies, got food, talked about every topic on this earth. Nothing was off limits, and nothing was awkward between us. Everything flowed. It felt right. One day, I found out about some things he was doing behind my back. It made me so sick to my stomach because those actions did not line up with the person that I knew.

I thought I knew him better than anyone else, but I did not know that side of him. I decided I could no longer have him as part of my life because of what happened. So, every day, I had to wake up without my best friend. Every day something happened that I wanted to tell him about. But I couldn't. I couldn't have someone in my life who had hurt me that much.

I sat and thought about all the memories we had, and how much I missed him. I didn't eat for days. I cried because I lose my best friend. Then I realized something, yes, he had been my best friend for about six years. Yes, we have so many memories together. What happened did not change our memories or the friendship we had. It just meant we could no longer have that friendship. Honestly, I did not want to be friends with someone who could hurt me so badly. Part of me was so sad that that chapter of my life was over, but the other part was so thankful that I didn't have to keep a friend who wasn't valuing me.

This may sound strange, but part of me was grateful that God loved me enough, not to allow me to keep relationships that hurt me. Grateful to find out what was going on, so I could find new people to surround myself with. I want to surround myself with honest and kind people, and those who value me.

I understand losing someone in your life is really hard. I was so angry about losing my best friend. I would have never chosen for that to happen to me. I honestly would never have chosen any of the hard things that have come my way. I am sure you feel the same. Sometimes I shake my fist at God in anger because things aren't the way I want them. They hurt, and I had a picture in my head about how things should be. But for some reason, that I don't know of, he has a plan. Where I am right now, and what I am going through, is exactly where I need to be.

Even though losing people is devastating, you can be grateful that now you can find other people who will treat you better and lift you up. You can let go of that old toxic friendship. Be grateful for it, grateful for the memories, and for the lessons it taught you about life, and about yourself. But be thankful that the things that hurt you are leaving your life even if their absence hurts. Instead of thinking to myself, "Why is this happening to me?" I started thinking, "What is this trying to teach me?"

Relationships are part of what makes us who we are. People are blessings or lessons in our lives, sometimes both. Everything we go through is to make us who we are supposed to be. Every hard thing you have ever faced or will face is a lesson to help you be who you are created to be. They make you stronger, kinder, more patient, understanding, and more relatable to other people.

If you had never experienced any kind of hurt, how would you be able to relate to other people who are hurting? I will tell you a few things that my hurt taught me. Feeling unwanted and unloved by my birth dad caused me never to want to make anyone else feel that way. Because of that, I include as many people as possible, whenever I can, and I always show love to everyone that I meet. I want each person I meet to know that they matter.

The hurt I have felt from not having real friends, not being spoken too kindly, and being bullied taught me what I wanted in a friend. It taught me how to be a very good friend. Their unkind words showed me how much it hurt to be spoken to that way. So, when I speak to people, I try to make sure what I say is kind, and I do my best to stop gossiping. I also try to stop bullying whenever I see it happen. I never want anyone to feel what I felt, and if they do, I let them know they can always talk to me about it.

My self-destructiveness and meanness to myself taught me that I have to be my own biggest fan. If I constantly talk down to myself, I will never be positive or in a good mood. I won't be able to be nice to others if I am not nice to myself. My toxic relationship with myself caused me to change and treat myself the best I can.

Everything that I have gone through with my birth dad, the girls at school, and struggles with myself has led me here. All of the nights that I cried myself to sleep have led me here. Every time I thought I couldn't get through something because it hurt too much, that led me here: to write this book. I would not be writing this book to try to help you if I had not gone through my hard times. I can look back and still feel the hurt of things that I have gone through, but also feel grateful that I went through them. I went through them, so I could help you. It was all for you. It was so that I could write this book, that this book would end up in your hands and that something in here would help you. That something I have gone through or that has helped me, can help your heart. That you can know that who you are is exactly enough, and you are not alone.

I wouldn't choose it, but I wouldn't change it.

If I can make it through, so can you. Our greatest treasure lies next to our deepest wound. The thing that hurt us the most is going to be used in our lives to help other people battle that same wound. Next time you are going through something, remember that it is to make you who you are. It hurts, and it sucks, and that is okay, but it is teaching you something. One day you will look back and be thankful for who that hard time made you become. Just remember, you are loved and if you feel like you've had enough — please talk to someone.

"I will continue to fight because I know I'll one day meet someone who isn't strong enough to fight the same battle I've won."

– Bela Fayth

Ideas to remember from this chapter:

1. What are three things you are grateful for?

    1. _____

    2. _____

    3. _____

2. What are two things you have gone through that can help other people?

_____

_____

_____

_____

_____

_____

_____

_____

_____

_____

3. What is something that has hurt you, but taught you a lesson that you are grateful for?

_____

_____

_____

_____

_____

_____

_____

4. Think of one person you can help with your story.

_____

_____

_____

_____

_____

_____

_____

5. Each day this week I want you to think of two things every morning that you are grateful for. List them here:

_____

_____

_____

_____

_____

_____

_____

_____

Bela's Answers

1. • My mom
   • Books
   • Sleep

2. • My battle with my self-worth.
   • My struggle with boundaries and people pleasing.

3. Losing friends that are close to me has hurt my heart, but it has taught me how to be a good friend and what to look for in good friends.

4. My little sisters.

CHAPTER TWELVE
Validation

> Validation
> *noun*
> 1. recognition or affirmation that a person or their feelings or opinions are valid or worthwhile.

Have you ever gone through something and wanted someone to see your side of things? Have you wanted someone to take the time and say, "Man, I'm sorry that sounds really hard"? Or maybe you thought you had a great idea and you wanted to hear, "Dang that is such a great idea!" Both of these are examples of validation.

Validation feels good. It lets us know we are on the right path and we are doing something right, or we are feeling something valid. We talked a bit about validation during the feelings chapter. I told you that whatever you are feeling is okay. There is no right or wrong way that you should be feeling. You feel what you feel.

A lot of times in my life I did not receive validation from the people I wanted it from. I wanted my birth dad to see that he sucked, and he was hurting me. I wanted those girls to be better friends and see that the way they were treating me went straight to my heart. I felt like I would try to do things to gain other people's validation. Instead of being myself, I started living for others approval, so I could fit in, and I could feel good about myself.

I would go along with the crowd, and I wouldn't speak up. I would keep my feelings to myself. I would avoid conflict. I wouldn't say "no." I would do so many things that did not align with who I was, just to get some validation. Seeking someone's validation in a way that hurts yourself, or changes who you are is not validation. It is instant gratification, which is a fancy way of saying you want approval and you want it now.

Another place I have seen the presence of instant gratification is on social media. We use filters. We post one out of one hundred selfies — never the bad ones. We only post the pictures we look skinny in. We want people to comment on our pictures and tell us how pretty we are, so then maybe, just maybe, we will believe it ourselves. Wouldn't it be nice just to think you are pretty and love who you are, regardless of what people think?

Validation is simply knowing or being told that it's okay. You feel like crying because someone said something mean to you? I totally get that; I would feel like crying too. You get mad at your mom because she always seems to know better and doesn't really listen to you? I'm sorry. That sucks. I hate when moms do that. You feel like your friends don't hear you when you talk? That is one of the worst things. What you have to say is important, even if they don't think so. I just validated all of those things. Not just for examples, but for real. Whatever you are going through is okay. NO one should tell you what you should or should not feel.

I have realized that adults sometimes seriously suck at validation or don't understand it. I learned that this is because, as we get older, our problems get bigger. Instead of being sad because someone said they didn't like your shirt, adults get sad and worried about bills, jobs, kids, things like that. So, to them, when we come home from school crying about what someone said to us, not being invited to a party, or the boy who doesn't like us back, it isn't that big of a deal to THEM. A lot of times they don't remember what being our age was like. But that does not mean that the hurt you are feeling is not important, because it is.

You have to remember that our parents are seasoned. They have already been through all of this. They forget how much it hurts when you feel things for the first time. They tell you to "Just get over it" or to "Toughen up." I am here to tell you that it is okay to be hurt no matter how "silly." Other people don't have to agree with your feelings, because they are YOURS. You feel how you feel. I know how much you want your parents, friends, or that boy to understand. "If they could just see things through my eyes or feel them with my heart, they would understand." I used to say this all the time because I wanted validation.

I realized that the person I needed validation from the most, was myself. If I told myself that how I was feeling was okay, then I was more okay with it. If I told myself, "Man, I am having a rough day." I would acknowledge that it had been hard instead of pretending and trying to be "fine."

I don't know if you have ever pretended that something was fine when it wasn't. But I got to be really good at it. It was exhausting. Then one day I just got tired of it, and I started to validate and feel my feelings. I did not let them decide for me or run my life. I felt them, but I controlled them. You are not your thoughts or feelings. You are what you do with them.

Think of how much it means to you when you are validated. Sometimes you want to just talk to someone without hearing their opinions. You simply want them to listen and validate what you are going through. You don't always need advice, but just someone to hear you. You want to be reminded that your thoughts matter, your voice and what you have to say matters. What you are feeling matters. You like knowing others care. Knowing how much it means to you, you should try to be that person for other people too.

If you have a friend talking to you about something she is struggling with, just listen, hear her, and validate her. It will build her up and remind her that she matters and that everything will be okay. Or maybe next time you want to be heard, you could ask your friend, mom, aunt, cousin, or whoever to just *listen* to you. Tell them that they don't need to give you advice, or fix it, but just to hear what you have to say.

When you feel like you are not seen or heard it affects everything. What you think about yourself, how you carry yourself, how you treat others, everything. I get it, I've been there. I know what it feels like when you feel like you don't matter or that something is wrong with you. I am here to tell you that what you say matters. What you think matters. Your dreams matter. Your decisions matter. How you feel matters. Your mental health matters. You matter. You are you, and that is your superpower. No one else will ever be able to be who you are. Own the things that make you, you. Own your voice, your feelings, your thoughts, own who you are. You were created for a reason. You matter.

Ideas to remember from this chapter:

1. Where do you notice instant gratification in your life?

_____

_____

_____

_____

_____

_____

_____

_____

2. What needs to be validated in your life?

_____

_____

_____

_____

_____

_____

_____

_____

3. Who do you seek validation from the most?

_____

_____

_____

_____

_____

_____

_____

4. Take time to write yourself a letter validating yourself, and how you feel.

_____

_____

_____

_____

_____

_____

_____

Bela's Answers

1. I see instant gratification the most in my life on social media. I double check with myself why I am posting what I'm posting to make sure its not for attention or validation. Sometimes it is.

2. I need to validate that I am good enough and that I am exactly where I'm supposed to be. I tend to put pressure on myself to do more or be more.

3. I tend to seek validation the most from my mom. Her opinion really matters to me.

4. Dear Bela,

I know you are feeling overwhelmed and not good enough and thats okay. Take things one day at a time and be kind to yourself. You are doing the best you can.

I am proud of you.

I love you.

♡ Bela.

CHAPTER THIRTEEN

Self-Love

> Self-Love
> *noun*
> 1. regard for one's own well-being and happiness

I am writing this with tear-stained eyes.

I have been putting off writing this chapter. Before this, I wrote some cookie cutter sugar coated version that was not me. It was not raw. It wasn't real. But I am scared for the real chapter. I am scared to talk to you about self-love, when right now, at this moment, I do not want to love myself.

My normal was ripped from me not too long ago. I am sure you've had your normal torn away a time or two. Whether it was losing your best friend since kindergarten, breaking up with a boy that you wanted to be "the one," maybe having a parent decide not to parent anymore, or realizing that something wasn't what you thought it was. I don't know what you are going through, but it hurts.

Do you remember in the gratitude chapter, when I talked about losing my best friend? He and I had been best friends since sixth grade. We talked about everything; we would often stay up all night talking on the phone. We always had each other's back, no matter what.

As we got older, our feelings for each other grew stronger. I had liked him for years, I just lied to myself about it because the thought of losing my best friend terrified me. Finally, after he had chased me for four years, I said "yes" and became his girlfriend.

Today, as I write this on a quiet Sunday afternoon, it has been four months since I found out I wasn't the only girl he was seeing. It's been four months since my normal, and everything I thought to be true was ripped out from under me, and I felt like I was hit by a bus with all sorts of emotions hitting me at once.

I came home from church today and saw the empty spot on the couch where we use to take our after-church naps together, and my heart became heavy. It was part of my normal. Talking to him every day, calling him to tell him about something exciting that happened, hanging out with him, joking around with him, and being in his arms. These things were all part of my normal. I can no longer do any of these things.

I would be lying to you if I said I was over it. It would also be lying to you to tell you that I want better for myself. Because I don't. I get so angry that every-thing is different. I feel raged that it can never go back to the way it was. My heart aches with memories of how things were. I miss it. I miss my normal. I feel guilty for missing it, for being mad, and for choosing every day to wake up and do what's best for me. What is best for me now, is not my normal because my normal was toxic for me. We might never be okay with our normal, or what has happened to us, and we don't have to be. We just have to accept it and go from there, one day at a time.

I don't know what your normal is or was. But I get it. I get not wanting things to change, not wanting to move on, or wanting to skip the pain and be healed already. I also get not wanting to love yourself because when you chose to love yourself, you do what's best for you, even if it hurts like you've never hurt before.

That's how I feel right now. I know what self-love is, I know why it is important, and I still have a hard time believing in it and living it out. When I feel like this, I cry. Honestly, I cried to my mom while sitting on top of the toilet before writing this chapter.

Loving what is does not mean that you don't get angry, feel like punching a wall, screaming, crying, crying some more, feeling confused, or whatever you are feeling. Loving what is gives you permission to feel all those emotions and accept that things change.

Even though things change, we can get to a place where the love we have for ourselves doesn't. Self-love looks different for everyone. First, you have to pay attention to the things that make you feel loved, happy, or full of joy.

Some examples are:
- working out
- going on runs
- coffee
- journaling
- taking a bath
- taking a nap
- hanging out with friends
- buying yourself flowers
- praying
- listening to music

Acts of self-love do not have to be big; they just have to remind you that you matter.

I believe having self-love is having true confidence. True confidence is showing up as yourself, in every situation. It is choosing to love who you are, exactly how you are. For me, right now, I am choosing to love myself with no makeup and with puffy tear-stained eyes and a heavy heart.

True confidence does not mean that you don't have insecurities or moments where you don't like yourself. Let me tell you a secret, *everyone* you will ever meet, has insecurities AND moments where they don't like themselves.

Here are some ways to help you be more truly confident:

- Keep the promises you make to yourself.
- Allow yourself to feel how you feel.
- Compliment instead of comparing.
- Find things you like about yourself, and focus on those more than the things you dislike.
- Speak to yourself with love (hello, self-talk!)
- Do what you KNOW is right.
- Surround yourself with honest, loving people.
- Say "no" and set boundaries.
- Take time for yourself.

The road towards being truly confident is one you have to take steps on each day. It happens moment by moment, choice by choice. You can choose to be falsely confident or truly confident. Being either is hard. It takes a lot of effort to be negative, hating on yourself and others all the time. But it takes the same amount of energy to choose to love yourself and be kind to others. Whichever one you spend the most effort on is the one you will be. One choice can change everything.

Having true confidence is being able to change things you don't like. These past couple of days you have been negative and mean to yourself? That's okay. Think one kind thought about yourself and do better today. Yesterday you gossiped about one of your friends? Okay, apologize and do better today. You've been comparing yourself on social media? Alright, take some time to write affirmations and do better. There is nothing that you have done or ever will do that you cannot bounce back from. It starts with one choice to do better.

Self-love and the choices you make are important because they affect everything in your life like:

- how you carry yourself
- how you talk to yourself
- how you treat others
- the way you play sports
- how well you do in school
- how you bounce back from mistakes.

Your self-talk is a huge part of self-love. If you think you will fail this math test and you think that you suck at math, you won't be acting out of true confidence. You will second guess yourself and chances are you will suck on the math test. *You will always give yourself what you think you deserve.* If you don't think highly of yourself, you won't think you deserve very much. You get to choose each morning how you are going to live.

Something that can affect our self-love as well is social media. Have you ever seen someone post a picture and their boobs were hanging out, or maybe it was their butt, or maybe they are in a surprising pose? Have you seen a post like that?

A couple of years ago, there were girls at my school who regularly posted stuff like that. The majority of people have social media, so the majority of people saw what they were posting. Part of me wanted to post just like them. I have a nice body, and I wanted to be noticed and seen. I wanted to be wanted. Like others, I wanted attention, and I thought that maybe I had to post like that to get it.

Thankfully my mother and I have a relationship where I can talk to her about anything, so I told her about my struggle. I told her that I knew it wasn't right, but I wanted to post pictures like that also. I felt like if I didn't then maybe I wasn't as good or attractive as the girls who did. Maybe boys wouldn't want me as much as they wanted those girls. She reminded me that whatever I post online, will never go away. Would I want my grandma to see photos like that of me? How do I think of myself? When I thought more about it, my heart hurt for the girls who thought that in order to be loved, seen, or noticed, they had to post pictures like that. My heart hurt for myself that I thought I had to as well.

A particular girl in my grade posted a ton of photos like that. I was in the school library one day and heard the counselor talking about inappropriate pictures that were being printed by some of the students, and they happened to be her exposing pictures. I remember that the girl was so upset and angry that someone would print her pictures at school. She was angry that she got in trouble because of it. I just remembered thinking, "man that sucks, but if you don't want everyone to see it, why post it?" I understand loving your body because I love my own. I don't understand having to post pictures to PROVE that you love your body. In my opinion, you don't need to prove what is true. It isn't what you do that shows your self-love, but how you do it.

Self-love is not only being confident when you have your hair and makeup all done, and you have a bomb outfit on or when everything is going well in life. Anyone can get dressed up and feel pretty. It is fun. Anyone can be happy when everything is going well. But self-love is about loving who is underneath. The girl without the makeup, the girl in sweats and a sweatshirt. The girl with the frizzy hair, the girl who dances around and jams in her room. The one who randomly bursts out into songs. The girl with tears in her eyes. The girl who is going through a hard time right now but is doing her best. The girl who is fighting to be better. That girl, I like that girl.

I still struggle with what self-love is. There are so many different explanations out there for what it is. Sometimes I think I am just going to wake up and magically love myself fully. Sadly, that is not how it works. I learned that I have to wake up each day, and moment-by-moment choose whether I am going to build myself up or tear myself down. I will never wake up one day and just be confident. I will have to choose how I want to treat myself and others that day, or sometimes even that *moment*. It takes practice, and the more you and I act a certain way, the easier it is.

Sweet girl, you cannot hate yourself and love others. You cannot hate yourself and treat others right. You cannot hate yourself and do what is best for you. You cannot love and accept others without first loving and accepting yourself. This does not mean that you don't hurt, get angry, have hard days, or get annoyed at the way things are going in your life. It means that despite all of that, you still love yourself and you do your best to be better each day.

Some days it will be harder to love yourself than other days. I know, I totally get it. All we can do is our best. It is okay to have good days and hard days. Your best is enough. People will be mean, say rude things, and you cannot control what others choose to do. You can choose how you respond and how you are going to live. You can choose to affirm yourself and remind yourself who you are. OR you can respond out of false confidence and tear others down.

Will tearing others down really change anything for you? Will it fix the hurt or the insecurities you have? Will it make them go away? No, honey, it won't. Tearing others down doesn't make anything better, neither does talking about them, starting rumors, being mean, or embarrassing others. It is okay to be annoyed, hurt, angry, sad, whatever you feel is okay, but tearing someone else down because of how you feel, is not. They are still human; they hurt and feel all the same feelings you and I feel. They just have different experiences that gave them those feelings. Everyone on this planet matters and is loved.

You will be able to tell how someone treats and views themselves based on how they treat other people. If you are tearing someone down, you need to stop and look at the deeper problem or hurt that is causing you to act that way. If someone is tearing you down, you might need to take a step back and set some boundaries. When we listen to our feelings and validate them, we can decide what hurts our feelings. Just because we are all loved the same, doesn't mean you have to let anyone be a part of your life.

You can still love someone and be kind to them but set boundaries to protect your heart. Self-love is loving yourself enough to say "no" to the things and people that hurt you. It is removing yourself from harmful situations. It is saying "enough is enough, I am worth more and I won't settle for less than I deserve." This includes friends, boyfriends, girlfriends, self-talk, foods that make you sick, and anything that hurts you.

I wish I could take the hurt and the pain away from you. I wish I could take away the sleepless nights, where you can't stop crying. I wish I could take away the random memories that jab deep into your heart. I wish I could fix it and heal you. I wish I could make things go the way you want them too and make everything go back to normal. But I can't. And it hurts, and it sucks.

I get a lump in my throat and feel like crying often. It is life, and this life will have some pretty stinking hard days. Even though I can't do any of that for you, I can be there with you. I can relate. I can tell you to take things one day at a time. Each day you will heal a little and love yourself a little more. It is not about the destination; it is about the journey. This journey is the one where we become who we are made to be. It is the one where we love ourselves even when it hurts. It is the journey where we forgive those who hurt us, including ourselves.

This journey that we are on is our life. We will never be perfect; it is not about that. It is about being fully who we are. It is about growing through the hard things. It is about touching lives around us and letting people know that they are not alone. It is about standing in the middle of the mess and knowing that we will get through even the worst days that lay ahead of us because we have already gotten through the worst ones so far AND because we no longer have to go through them alone.

I see you.
The girl who walks with her head down.
The girl who dresses down, so others won't make fun of her.
The girl who laughs at her own jokes.
The girl who cares about those around her, more than she cares about herself.
The girl who wants to please everyone and make everyone happy.
The girl who is smiling, but behind that smile is pain.
The girl who doesn't really have any friends.
The girl who struggles with feeling her feelings.
The girl who struggles with comparison.
The girl who wants to be loved, seen, and enough.
The girl who wants to be strong, confident, and bold.
I see you because I am her too.

The God, who created heaven, earth, mountains, seas, and galaxies, decided that you and I needed to exist. We are enough, exactly who we are. Each day we will be better than who we were yesterday.

I pray that you will someday soon realize how loved you are, and I hope it overwhelms you and blows your mind. I pray that you will live in that love and give some of it to yourself and those around you.

Ideas to remember from this chapter:

1. Where in your life do you struggle with self-love?

_____

_____

_____

_____

_____

_____

_____

_____

2. What is something that you want to love more about yourself?

_____

_____

_____

_____

_____

_____

_____

3. What makes it hard for you to love yourself?

_____

_____

_____

_____

_____

_____

_____

_____

4. Write three things you love about yourself.

1. _____

2. _____

3. _____

Bela's Answers

1. I struggle with self-love after being rejected or left out. Sometimes I catch myself people pleasing to try to prove my worth. I have to remind myself I have nothing to prove and that people who are meant to be in my life, will be.

2. I want to be better at loving myself through hard moments. Instead of being hard on myself I want to be kind and validate myself.

3. Fear of not being enough, rejection, hurt, and comparison all are part of my struggle to love myself.

4. • My determination
   • My wisdom
   • The way I randomly quote movies.

CHAPTER FOURTEEN

A Letter

A Letter

Dear Friend,

Throughout this book, we have talked about a lot of things. We have talked about:

- The power of journaling, how it can help you process and deal with hard things, and also gives you a safe place.
- Realistic and unrealistic expectations, and how we set ourselves up to be disappointed.
- How other people rejecting us has nothing to do with us, and when we reject others, we are rejecting something in ourselves.
- How our feelings are always okay, but not always true. How to feel and communicate them.
- Self-talk and how it affects every area of our lives. How we speak to ourselves matters.
- The toxicity of comparison, and how it can steal our joy.
- How bullying is heartbreaking, and ways to help get through it.
- Protecting our hearts and listening to our guts to set personal boundaries for ourselves.

- How acceptance is acknowledging reality, and that you can still be hurt and bothered.
- What forgiveness is and isn't — unforgiveness is like drinking poison and hoping someone else dies.
- How we can have gratitude in every situation, even the ones that hurt the most, knowing it is making us who we were created to be.
- The fact that who you are and how you feel are both valid. You and everything you do matters.

I talked about all of these things because they are important and because I wish I would have known them earlier. Each of these topics has made a significant difference in my life, how I handle myself, and how I view myself. It is never what happens to you that makes you who you are. It is how you handle it.

How are you going to choose to handle the situation you are in right now? It sucks and hurts, and I am sorry. I know you can get through this. I know one day you will look back and it will all make sense why you had to go through this. Right now, you take it one day at a time.

Each day you wake up, you get to choose who you are. You get to choose what you will do, say, who you will hang out with, and how you are going to handle things that come your way. You are not helpless. You have a say in your life. You are the only person who gets to choose who you become. Each choice you make matters, and one choice is all it takes to change your life for better or worse. Try your best to be better than who you were yesterday. Write affirmations, remind yourself who you are. This earth needs exactly who you are. Let's change the world by being 100% ourselves every day. You've got this. You are enough. You are not alone. You are loved. I am cheering for you.

The last chapter of this book was by far the hardest to write. At first, I was terrified to be vulnerable and honest as I promised you. It turns out that it is my favorite chapter. You're almost done with the journey of this book, and I really hope some things in here helped you and have made a difference in your life. That is my biggest wish.

Sending all my love,

Bela

Take some time to write down a few things you have learned from this book. Then write a letter encouraging and validating yourself.

_____

_____

_____

_____

_____

_____

_____

_____

_____

_____

_____

_____

_____

_____

_____

_____

_____

ABOUT THE AUTHOR

Bela Fayth is the oldest of six, born and raised in Southern Minnesota. She has a big heart for people and helping them however she can. She loves music, dancing, being goofy, watching movies, reading, and trying new things. She is an author and a speaker. Bela's goal is to help millions of girls flourish as they navigate their preteen and teenage years.

For more information:
belafayth.com
@belafayth

Dear Reader,

   I am beyond thankful that my book ended up in your hands or in the hands of someone you love. I hope something in this book has made a difference in the life of the reader and everyone they come into contact with.

While I am passionate about changing lives through this book, I am determined to touch as many lives as possible. So in addition to this book finding it's way into as many hands as possible, making a personal face to face impact is something I am also passionate about doing. Speaking to various schools, organizations, and churches allows me the opportunity to meet with individuals and connect on a much deeper level.

I would love the opportunity to speak. If you or someone you know would be interested in having me share my insight, please email me at Belafayth@gmail.com to further discuss.

Thank you for the role you play in my mission to make an impact on this world.

     With love,

          Bela.

CPSIA information can be obtained
at www.ICGtesting.com
Printed in the USA
BVHW060023120220
572028BV00015B/1674